COUNTRY WAYS
& DIFFERENT DAYS

by Hamish Watt

Aberdeen Journals Ltd.

First published by
Aberdeen Journals Ltd., Lang Stracht,
Mastrick, Aberdeen AB9 8AF

ISBN 1 901300 04 8

Printed by Inglis Allen, Falkirk

ABOUT THE AUTHOR

Hamish Watt is a Keith loon who got his education at the local school and at St Andrews University, where he studied Economics.

After three years as aircrew in the R.A.F. he commenced farming in the North-East and quickly became immersed in local affairs and in agricultural politics.

He entered the political field as a Conservative when he contested Caithness and Sutherland at the 1966 General Election. This experience fostered his abiding love of the North.

After switching allegiance to the Scottish National Party, he won the Banffshire seat in February and October 1974 and served at Westminster for five years, three of them as Whip.

His subsequent career in local politics at both district and regional levels, plus his farming activities meant frequent burning of the midnight oil. He found the Chairmanship of the Education Committee particularly challenging and rewarding.

Three years as Rector of Aberdeen University from 1986 led to him being awarded an honorary doctorate.

Early contributions to Farm Journal resulted in Hamish being allocated a weekly column where along with his great friend and rival, Charlie Allan, they share their wit and wisdom with Saturday readers.

FOREWORD

The catalogue of writers who have portrayed the rural life of the North-east is long and distinguished. The contributions of the men and women who have written about the cold shoulder of Scotland are at the same time varied in depth, approach and style.

Names like Lewis Grassic Gibbon and John R. Allan spring to mind instantly, but there is a host of others, some perhaps less well known, who have formed part of the rich pantheon of prose.

Writers like Dr John B. Pratt offered a tantalising picture of Buchan a century ago, while the journalist, William Alexander produced several underrated studies of the land and the people against the social, political and religious backcloth of the mid nineteenth century.

Hamish Watt, with his second collection of essays, personal reminiscences and anecdotes has now laid claim effectively to being ranked among those who shone a particular and distinctive light on the ways, foibles and characteristics of the people who live and work the land.

Hamish Watt never set out to make such a claim, but his weekly contributions to *The Press and Journal* over the past years have clearly established him as a writer with a real and uncluttered insight into a way of life which is particularly rooted in the soil of the region.

The strength of Hamish Watt's writing lies not only in his empathy with agriculture and the problems and perils of eking a living from what can be, at times, a grudging soil, but in his ability to offer contributions and observations to which people can relate.

He has managed to draw extensively on his own fruitful, personal hinterland and his experience as a farmer, local and national politician, and man with a deep and transparent love of the countryside, and harness those strands in a variety of illuminating sketches.

Because he speaks the local language so well and mirrors the views and thoughts of so many of the people he has come into contact with, his writing maintains the freshness, vitality and charm that can be such elusive qualities. To do as he does, and write on a weekly basis in a sustainable way, is the real test of a skilled and sensitive wordsmith. Hamish Watt at the same time entertains, enrages, informs and provokes. It is no easy task but he has consistently shown that he is up to it.

The other major appeal of Hamish Watt's writings is his ability to tap that rich seam which is in essence a dialogue between the present and the past. His pieces on the feeing markets of yore, Gowk's corn, and the dominie are testimony to this, while many others reveal the practical farmer facing everyday problems. Others, like his memories of Harold Wilson, unveil the political eye, and a feel for that world. Many more in this collection simply expose a strong feeling of humanity.

It is perhaps the final theme that binds Hamish Watt's work together so powerfully. He has turned the spotlight on his own family in a way that is neither sentimental nor sugary, but is warm and appealing. His appeal: "if only as adults, we could retain some measure of a child's pleasure, energy and enthusiasm...life would indeed remain a great adventure" is a timely and poignant piece of home grown philosophy which can only be commended in this cynical world. It is Hamish Watt's passion for life that shines through these pages eloquently and elegantly.

Taken as a whole, this second collection of Hamish Watt's writing stands shoulder-to-shoulder with the first. It is a formidable slice of social history, and a colourful expression of an individual's view of the life and times in which he lives, as well as representing an important link in the on-going and fascinating story of life on the land.

As someone who for years edited Hamish Watt's prose for *The Press and Journal* (a task which was so undemanding as to constitute a joy), I am particularly pleased to have been asked again to provide this foreword.

BILL HOWATSON

Magical moment in Buchan

The smell curled roon my hairt like a hairy worm. I had stopped in New Pitsligo for some shopping and the moment I opened the car door I caught the glorious tang of peat reek. I stood for a while and just savoured it.

Unlike so many smells in the countryside nowadays, and unlike many scents that both men and women wear, peat reek has none of the harshness of artificial odours. Nothing quite matches it.

As I drank in the aroma, memories came flooding back. Peat reek was one of the first familiar, comforting smells of my childhood days. Our farm kitchen had an open fire with two sways for hanging pots on.

Although sticks were used in large quantities, peats provided the principal source of heat. Some coal was burned in the sittingroom, but never that I can remember in the kitchen.

A small recessed peat house at the side of the fire held three-and-a-half barrow loads of dried peats. I know, because I had to fill it often enough. When Monday washday came round, the wee shed was totally emptied and the peat dross used to bank up the fire so that there would be plenty of hot water for the huge wash of family clothes, dairy and byre overalls.

Cleaning out that peat sheddie was a big job for a three-year-old. Many a time I curled up in the cupboard with the door shut and fell fast asleep. Luckily, I always wakened in time for dinner and the milk-rice soup that was as much a part of Mondays as the wash itself.

Winning the peats was hard work, but at least they were a cheap source of fuel. A rural area with no peat moss within horse-carting distance could experience big problems.

For example, the parish of Cairnie, near Huntly, suffered real hardship when the local mosses were worked out. Many families were forced to migrate in search of a fuel supply. The coming of the railway proved a godsend in making coal available for those who could afford it.

A fair proportion of mosses contained poor quality or foggy peat. Little better than turf, it burned quickly when dry and produced far less heat than the real black peat. And it definitely did not give off the same lovely aroma.

I sometimes wonder if Aberchirder became familiarly and famously known as Foggieloan because the local moss produced dour, foggy peats. Apparently, the moss of Crombie in Marnoch was the preferred source of supply for the villagers, even although it was some distance away. Distilleries always had the privilege of working the very best part of any moss, but likely they paid sweetly for it. They needed the reek to give flavour to their whiskies.

Peat mosses were owned by the lairds, and they could be very choosy about granting permission to extract. Annually, on a specific day in spring, a lair was allocated to each farm and croft on the estate; and from then until the peats were securely stacked, the calender of events followed a strict pattern.

Immediately after the turnip crop was sown, the peats were cut and cast up on to the bank above the diggings. Most years it was necessary to remove a slab of

turf from the top of the lair, and this was either trampled into the bottom of the diggings or used to repair the rough tracks out of the moss.

When the neeps had been hoed, it was back to the moss to barrow the slightly dried peats to a point nearer the road. Then, between cutting and colling the hay, they were set on their ends to dry out thoroughly, with a heavy wet one placed across the top. Care had to be taken in setting peats because rough handling could break them into small pieces.

Finally, if it had been a reasonably dry summer and all had gone well, the loads were carted home in the period between the end of hay-making and the start of harvest.

It was hard graft at the best of times, but especially so in a wet season. A prolonged rainy spell meant that the peats could not be cast, and shifting them from the bank where they'd been cut to a convenient lair to dry was heavy work. The peat barrows soon tired the most willing men and women.

Still, "mossing" had its compensations. There was the close camaraderie of folk from various farms getting together. There was the bonnie sight of the soft, white bog cotton waving in a summer breeze. And above all, there was the extra special taste of moss tea – a special brew produced in a billy can over a peat fire.

On the other hand, there were the midgies. Every movement of every peat raised up a swarm of the brutes. There never was a midgie yet that could resist the smell of perspiration on a human body, and a peat moss on a hot, windless day was sheer murder.

Less lethal than the midgies, but unpleasant enough, were the huge black beetles that lodged in the dry peats and had a nasty habit of crawling out on you when the cart was being loaded. I used to encounter a few when filling and cleaning out my wee peat shed, too, and they were nae a bairn's best companions.

Another recollection from childhood concerns an incident in the late summer of 1936. I had just returned to school after a long illness and I'd little pith. One day at about a quarter to four, I was thrilled to hear the unmistakable sound of horses and carts pulling heavy loads of peats up the steep brae past Keith Grammer School. The large number suggested to me that they were almost certainly from our farms, and the prospect of throwing my bike on top of a load and getting a ride home was very sweet.

As soon as the bell went, I cycled furiously and caught up with the carts just in time to witness a disaster. Each man with his two horses was driving with slack reins and paying little attention. Each horse had its head over the cart in front. Suddenly, the lead mare stopped to answer the call of nature. Every one of the following horses crashed into the preceding cart and the lightly-constructed peat creels were smashed to bits.

Spars, peats and harness flew everywhere as fourteen carts telescoped like cars in a motorway fog. So, far from getting my longed-for rest, I had to run about fetching timber and nails, wire and rope for the running repairs.

The housewives on the street had a bonanza among the scattered peats. I wonder if they enjoyed the aroma of that peat reek as much as I enjoyed the magical smell in New Pitsligo last week.

Goodies from the girdle!

"She's nae a scone of yesterday's baking." That was how my mother used to describe a lady who was wearing on in years.

On reflection, I think she always made the comment in respect of single ladies and – most unfairly – never applied the description to a man of similar age.

Anyway, yesterday's scones were still pretty tasty. Only after three or four days did they become tough and stale. In Ayrshire, no breakfast plate was complete without a fried scone to accompany the bacon and egg.

Monday afternoon was baking time. A huge zinc bathful of oatmeal, and on top of it a large linen cloth containing flour, was carried the hundred yards to the bothy.

The Aga cooker could not cope with the numbers of oatcakes and scones required to satisfy the daily needs of some twenty people with hearty appetites. And so the large open fire in the bothy, with its two sways for hanging girdles, was pressed into service each week.

The fire of sticks and peats would have been burning for at least two hours by the time baking started. The first blaze having died down, a steady, even heat provided ideal conditions for using the girdle.

In addition to oatmeal and flour, salt, baking soda and cream of tartar were carried in the bath. Also transported to the bothy was one milk churn containing whey for mixing with the oatmeal. At some farms plain water was used, but we generally had whey left over from Sunday's making of crowdie (cottage cheese, as it is now known).

Nowadays, all milk is collected by the milk-marketing board's huge road tankers. The milk-marketing board came late to Banffshire. When Aberdeenshire and Kincardine set up their milk agency in 1933, Banffshire opted out and did not join the board until wartime, at the insistence of the Ministry of Food. As a result, every dairy farmer in our area during the thirties had to find a way to utilise the milk he had surplus to retail round requirements.

Sunday's milk sales were always less than those on weekdays, and the resultant surplus was turned into butter and this delicious crowdie. The by-products – buttermilk and whey – were then used for Monday's baking session. We wasted nothing, thanks largely to the managing skills of my mother.

The oatcakes were baked first. Oatmeal, salt and whey were mixed together, then rolled thin on a flat baking board that had been sprinkled with dry oatmeal so that the round oatcake would slide easily onto the hot girdle.

Our girdle was twenty-four inches in diameter and the flat, raw oatcake covered it. To prevent the mixture from sticking to the hot metal, the girdle surface was rubbed with fat between each batch.

Immediately the mixture was on the girdle, my mother scored it with a big knife into six slices only – big oatckes for big appetites. Then every slice had to be turned with a spatula. It usually took two hours steady going to get all the oatcakes baked.

A start was then made to the scones. The fire was stoked up again for a fast bake. Flour, salt, baking soda, cream of tartar and liberal amounts of buttermilk had been mixed earlier. This mixture was pounded on a well-floured baking board, rolled and turned and rolled again.

When the doughy bannock was nearly the size of the girdle surface, it was carefully slid onto the well-greased girdle. When slightly baked, it was cut into eight pieces and each of these were flipped over to bake the other side. It was lovely to see the mixture rise, although the scones never rose so spectacularly as girdle pancakes.

Scones were best eaten the first or second day when the baking soda in them was still fresh. There was something akin to magic about the way a scone and rhubarb jam would fizz in your mouth. They never tasted better than when eaten with sweet hot cocoa in the lea of a stook in the harvest field.

Poorly-made scones were something else. It must have been awful for a farmhand to be fee-ed at a farm where the kitchie deem couldn't bake.

On the daily milk-delivery round both milkman and horse were very often offered a piece. For a time I had a cross Clydesdale mare called Bess that literally lived for her pieces. She would mount the pavement and rattle doorknobs with her nose to attract attention. Children loved feeding her, and I'm sure many a mother could have seen that horse far enough.

Sometimes, if she was nearing one of her "piece" doors she wouldn't stop on command. Wandering forward on her own was all very well when traffic was light, but it was a bit hair-raising when there were parked cars around.

But there was one door she never stopped at, although she got a piece each baking day. The housewife would present both Bess and myself with a scone, always remarking: "There's naething like a bit o' hame baking" – and there wasn't!

I was forced to politely agree, say "thank you" and take a bite out of mine. Bess hadn't learned manners, though, and just spat hers out. I used to make the excuse that she had already eaten too many pieces, and I would assure the lady that Bess would get her treat later. In fact, nothing would induce the mare to eat these scones at any time. The scones which were offered were always newly baked, but the housewife, kind soul that she was, just didn't have the knack. It was as if she had substituted cement for cream of tartar.

The finished product might have done service as causey stanes, but they were totally inedible to this milkman and his beast.

Packman days are gone

Farms are lonely places nowadays.

Fewer travellers call than ever before. There are two reasons for this. The recession has sent several agricultural firms to the wall, and the number selling fertilisers, chemical sprays or animal feedstuffs has declined at an alarming rate over the past five years.

Secondly, the farmer is seldom anywhere near the house or steading. Since he is often the only worker about the place, it's a fair bet that he will be off in a distant field working on a tractor.

Many of the callers of yesteryear have disappeared completely from the rural scene. The scrap dealer, the packman, the grocer's cart and the baker's van – all have gone the way of the dodo.

When there were chiels in the bothies and lasses in the farm kitchen, a packman's visit was quite an occasion. He usually did brisk business in scarves, neckties, jumpers and materials.

His wooden box, slung over one shoulder with a broad leather strap, contained thread, wool, pins, tiepins, thimbles and all sorts of trinkets. Over his other shoulder he carried a long roll of materials wrapped in waterproof oilskin to protect the goods from sun and rain.

The cheap-jack always opened his box first, and only after everyone had chosen what they required would he condescend to unravel his roll. He would spread it out on a bothy bed to reveal layer after layer of materials all tightly wrapped together.

There would be a length or two of tweed on the outside. Inside that were lengths of worsteds suitable for making up into trousers or skirts. The next layer consisted of coloured cottons, while in the very centre would be gaudy silks. It was a poor day indeed if the packman didn't make a sale of some kind.

The advent of World War II marked the end of the walking or cycling packman. After the war, these familiar characters were replaced by itinerant drapers with vans – many from the sub-continent of India.

I used to have a charming Pakistani gentleman who parked his van overnight in our farm close and slept among his merchandise. On every visit, he bought a hen from me and killed, plucked and prepared it in an open-front shed. I would come from the house to check the cattle after finishing a tasty tea, and the gorgeous aroma of cooking chicken and oriental spices made me hungry all over again.

As well as the Pakistani selling drapery, local drapers' vans also called at farms. This mixture of callers gave rise to a lovely story from Caithness. The local draper in Wick (who, incidentally, delighted in telling this story about himself) was very active in civic affairs and widely known and respected throughout the community.

On Wednesday afternoons, when his shop was shut and his vanman had a day off, he went round the rural areas himself. Drawing up at the back of a farmhouse one day, he found a little lad of about four sitting on the doorstep. "Is your mammy in?" the draper asked. "Yes," replied the youngster, staying firmly on the step. "Well, will you tell her I'm here?" said the draper. Reluctantly, the boy got up, opened the door and shouted: "Mam, here's the white darkie."

Grocers' vans were always welcomed by the bairns at farms because they offered a mesmerising variety of jars, tins and bottles full of goodies. As the range of products expanded after the war, new items were added to the traditional farm grocery list. This could have its problems for those unfamiliar with the new-fangled tastes.

A grocery vanman who gave a quarter of a century's service to the farming community before he retired once told me of an amusing encounter with a customer in the mid 1950s.

Wullie was a conscientious farmhand but just that bittie slow on the up-take and, unfortunately, afflicted with a harelip which impaired his speech. This particular day, the farmer's wife was occupied with some newly-orphaned lambs, and she asked Wullie to get her messages from the grocer when he called.

The vanman filled up the basket and when it came to Wullie's apparent request for toffee, he inquired which sort the farmer's wife preferred. More than a little irritated at what seemed to be the grocer's stupidity, Wullie growled: "Toffee? Nae toffee, man. Coffee – the stuff for makin' tea."

Another great story concerns the day a farmer's wife in Upper Banffshire was entertaining some non-farming ladies to afternoon tea. She warned her two young sons to stay outside and "keep oot o' the wey".

It happened to be shortly after the sheep clipping and, as chance would have it, the local scrap merchant called to collect the bags of claggings, daggings and broken wool. There were no menfolk around, so the scrappie asked the boys if their mother was in the house. The eldest opened the parlour door where his mother was taking tea with the minister's wife, the banker's wife and one or two other genteel ladies. The work of the farm was a lot more important to him than fancy china and post hats, so without a moment's hesitation he bawled out: "Hey, mam! Here's the mannie for the sh★★★y 'oo" (wool).

Another factor making for less lively atmosphere on farms is the steadily diminishing size of farming families. Whereas I had plenty of brothers and sisters to make up a playing squad when we were young, my two grand-daughters have to recruit their father and even their grandfather to play games like hide-and-seek, corners, and pop goes the weasal.

The other evening just before teatime, the girls managed to get their dad and myself out of our chairs for a game of ring-a-roses. After a few fall downs, the six-year-old felt she had to go to the bathroom. Shortly after, the four-year-old decided she had better go too. Solemnly, she announced: "You two just play on by yourselves until we come back."

I supposed she will have to be an adult herself before she understands why the two of us collapsed helpless with laughter.

Farm folk's feast of brose and bannocks

It will soon be Brose and Bannock Day, or if you prefer it, Shrove Tuesday or Fastern's E'en.

For people in French-speaking countries it is Mardi Gras, while Latin countries know the festival as Carnival.

I wonder if Shrove Tuesday was the origin of the phrase "that's a moveable feast", because it rarely falls on the same day two years running. The dates of Shrove Tuesday and of Ash Wednesday are ruled by the phases of the moon, just as surely as are the tides of the sea. An old rhyme confirms it:

First comes Candlemas, and syne the new meen;
The first Tuesday efter that is aye Fastern's E'en.

Celebration of the eve or e'en before the fast of Lent has largely died out in the North of Scotland. I have had to jog memories of quite a few of my contemporaries and of older people to find out just how important a day it was in the lives of farm folk in the first half of this century. In previous centuries, of course, the festival had even greater significance.

The origins of Brose and Bannock Day go back to pagan times. As with so many other festivals, the early Christian Church craftily adopted the day and adapted it to suite their own purpose. By using established holidays, the early missionaries made the Christian message more acceptable to our wild, independent-minded ancestors.

Early man believed that Shrove Tuesday marked the end of nature's dormant period. It brought the first stirring of life in the seeds that would germinate and flourish when the land dried out.

Later, the church ordained it as the day upon which to use the eggs and fat foods which would be forbidden during Lent. Alternatively, the food could be distributed among the poor of the parish. But don't quote me as an authority on early church history.

Brose and Bannock Day was something of a special occasion in our home when I was a bairn. I can only just recall sitting on the long wooden bench with my short legs dangling under the wide, well-scrubbed kitchen table. The brose was made in the biggest baking bowl in the house – almost eighteen inches across the top.

It was so deep that I couldn't reach the brose after the first few spoonfuls had been taken out by the many spoons round the big table. Then I found that if I knelt on the bench I could reach farther over the table and successfully claim my fair share.

I have always been fond of brose. Over the years I've enjoyed oatmeal brose, pease brose, neep brose and kail brose. But none of these were as scrumptious as Brose and Bannock Day brose because it was made with beef stock. A piece of boiling beef and a bone had been gently simmered overnight to bring out the full flavour. The hot stock blended with the oatmeal produced an extra special taste and I needed no persuasion to obey the grace said at the beginning of the denner:

Grace be here and grace be there,
And Grace be on the table.

Let ilka ane tak up their speen
And sup a that they're able.

You wouldn't think it to see me now, but as a small boy I was always a "picker". Food just didn't interest me. But on Brose and Bannock Day there was an added incentive to sup up.

Concealed within the brose in the big bowl would be a ring, a button and, in our house, several silver threepenny bits, all carefully wrapped in greaseproof paper. Whoever got the ring was to be married first. Whoever got the button would not be married at all. And those who got the threepennies were just plain lucky.

During the last century Shrove Tuesday was observed as a general holiday in some Catholic parishes such as Glenlivet. On farms, only the minimum of work was done. It was still a public holiday until fairly recent times, and schools closed at dinner time.

The young boys and youths spent the afternoon playing ball. No limits were set to the number of players in the teams on that special day, and the goal posts were simply a roughly-defined area. The pitch was always much longer than a normal football pitch. It could be an entire field, or the whole length of a street.

On farms, the ball for the game was usually made from "Glesga Jock", a coarse open-weave hemp rope used for tying the thatch on the corn rucks. This ball was always the size of a man's head, again connecting the festival to pagan times when the head of a human sacrifice would have been the "ba".

The Shrove Tuesday game seems to bear a close similarity to the "Ba Game" still played in some Orkney towns on another day earlier in the year.

The girls and smaller children of the parish spent the afternoon going round neighbours' doors where they would expect to receive a bannock, a piece of candy characterise the festivals of Hallowe'en and Hogmanay. In each case, the origin of the speirin dates back to the days when the poor of a parish asked householders for spare food.

All the men I have spoken to seemed to enjoy best the bannock bit of Brose and Bannock Day. In the evening, they and the lassies gathered round a roaring fire where the girdle was liberally smeared with fat to prevent the mixture sticking. Each person had to pour their own bannock onto the girdle.

There was great praise for the artistic ones. Some of the lads' bannocks were a trifle rude, but it all added to the fun of the evening. When the lassies were busy pouring their bannocks, the young men would try to untie the strings of their aprons, their skirts or even their stays. Or so I'm told! If that kind of thing went on in our kitchen, I was too young to notice or to understand.

The pancake mixture differed from the normal by the addition of some oatmeal. This resulted in a bannock which was rougher than usual. It was also much thinner. We bairns rolled the bannocks while they were still hot, then we filled the roll with jam or syrup and it was a race to eat the sticky mess before it dripped onto the front of our jerseys.

I recall that some of the bannocks were "fatty pancakes", but I don't ever remember them being "sautey" bannocks as in McGintie's Meal and Ale. In fact, I've never tasted salty pancakes. Maybe I ought to indulge in more research with the ladies instead of only asking men for their memories.

For me, the bannocks bit of Brose and Bannock Day is largely forgotten, but the special taste of that special brose on that special Tuesday will always keep me reminded of my early childhood. On second thoughts, why should it remain just a memory? I'll buy some boiling beef this weekend. I've got plenty of oatmeal.

To Russia without love . . .

His many friends will be delighted to hear that Sir Maitland Mackie is working on his memoirs. They will make interesting reading.

In the meantime, I'd like to tell a story that I know will not be included in his book. It concerns the day he nearly took a man's life – mine.

It was my great good fortune in the 60s and early 70s to be part of the Aberdeen Milk Marketing Board delegation that attended the annual International Dairy Congress. The congress was held in a different country every year; and in 1972, if I remember correctly, Russia played host.

Maitland Mackie, the chairman; Michael Boyle, the general manager; and I worked hard, actively participating in the many committee meetings and seminars. Each of these international gatherings provided a sounding board for the latest ideas in dairying and in dairy-produce manufacture.

Milk is an extremely versatile product, and in addition to butters, cheeses and yogurts, there are many other products that have still to catch on in this country. The British taste doesn't stretch to the soured milk products common to Central Europe and the Near East.

Although he was chairman of a very small milk marketing board, Maitland Mackie was highly regarded in dairying circles. His wise judgment was greatly valued by the giants in the industry. He had a wonderful knack of drawing together the strands of a wide-ranging discussion and eventually achieving a consensus from opposing views.

After the hectic five days of congress business it was customary for the delegates – at their own expense – to go on tours of the host country. Mr Mackie and Mr Boyle and their wives had chosen a different tour from my wife and I, but we arranged to meet up at Yalta, on the Black Sea, before returning to Britain.

Our tour did not go well. The night train to Kiev was hot, uncomfortable and very late. The Intourist guide was sullen, our interpreter lazy, and the minibus driver was a stranger in the city. They all knew how to point out prestigious buildings, such as the Palace of Industrial Achievement and the Planetarium of Soviet Space Discovery, but when it came to the location of farm institutes, the city dairy or the large state farm close to Kiev, they didn't know, nor did they trouble to find out. At one of these locations we turned up four hours late to find, not surprisingly, that the institute directors had all gone home.

The hotels were comfortable but restaurant service was atrocious. One Australian delegate left the table after the soup course and went to his room to bath and shave. He returned to find the rest of us still waiting for the meat course. Apparently we had hit a bad time when the kitchen staff were changing shifts.

The microphones concealed in the bedroom didn't exactly encourage cordial relations. One was obvious in the curtain pelmet, while the other could be traced by the way it vibrated when you "pinged" a glass.

On the second day, we visted a state farm of 1,500 hectares. Coming down the farm road we met a team of six horses pulling a tractor to the steading. Obviously, there was no other tractor in working order. Our information sheet proudly declared that there were fourteen tractors on the farm. It didn't lie but it failed to state that most of them were, by that time, heaps of rusting scrap behind the dyke.

Now I am normally slow to anger, but the chronic delays and inefficiencies really got under my skin. I finally blew my top and threatened to report them all to the Intourist Board. I told them that in every other country there was a forenoon, an afternoon and an evening, but that Russia had managed to lose one of these every day I had been there. The row did result in better time-keeping, but, needless to say, relations

between guide and guided were strained and I kept wishing the holiday was over.

The following afternoon we were taken to see a beautiful garden of remembrance commemorating the heoric struggle of the Russian people against the German invaders during the World War II.

As I was quietly admiring the tomb of the unknown soldier, with its perpetual flame, two strong hands clamped onto my shoulders. "Oh no! This is it. I've been reported to the KGB. I'm being arrested." I froze stockstill, except for the shaking knees.

Every incident of the Russian visit flashed through my mind. All my criticisms had been justified, but I should have bitten my tongue instead of losing my temper. I was ready to protest that I was really a friend of Russia – full of admiration for the state's encouragement of talented children, for the way the trade unions looked after their sick and elderly (providing them with free holidays by the sea or in a country dachau) and for the rich agricultural resources. Yet I was sure they wouldn't listen to my excuses. I had dared to criticise one small shortcoming, and that would be enough.

Stories I'd read about Russian work camps came vividly to mind. I was petrified. Nobody spoke. I stood there for an eternity – frozen by sheer terror. The vice-like grip at my shoulders never slackened. I couldn't turn round to face my captors.

Then I heard a woman laugh. Only one woman laughed like that – Pauline Mackie. I managed to draw a breath, then ducked and spun round to see the grinning face of Maitland Mackie towering above me. Don't anybody ever do that kind of thing to me again. My heart couldn't stand it a second time.

These boots were made for working . . .

I don't believe in the law of averages. Not anymore.

I've been buying green wellies for at least ten years, and everytime one leaks I throw it away and put its companion on a shelf in the shed. The other day my left wellie gave me a wet foot so I went for a spare, only to find that the five on the shelf were all for the right foot.

It used to be said that pilfering in the docks was so bad that exporters of boots and shoes made up their first consignment exclusively of goods for the left foot, then sent off the right feet some time later. Evidently, what I need is a job lot of left feet and I'd be set up for life.

At a farm roup last summer, I noticed one of the "good lifers" who have come to live among us sporting one green wellie and one black. He was a source of considerable amusement to the locals, but I can understand his feelings and his logic.

Still, if we all followed his example the wellie factory workers would go on short time, so I'd better fork out my £22 for replacements. I could pay more – even three times as much – but all I'd get extra would be the stamp on the side or the fashionable tab at the back.

I like the basic green wellie because it can be washed both outside and inside. A thorough wash freshens the insides and, I think, makes them warmer. Personally, I take a size bigger than I need and wear an extra pair of socks to keep up the heat. One thing is sure, without wellingtons you can't get far on a dairy farm, what with water in the dairy, dubs on the field gates, and sharn wherever the cattle are.

The name "wellington" is derived from the first Duke of Wellington, but why this should be puzzles me because the Duke's boots were very different. His were long leather boots worn under the trousers. They incorporated a strap under the instep to pull the trousers tight and accentuate the trouser line.

Rubber wellingtons were first manufactured around 1924, and they had a canvas frame with several layers of rubber sprayed on. The early wellies were not very comfortable. Their linings often went into "lirks" and caused blisters on the wearer's heels. In wet or wintry weather, most people continued re soft, squelchy, cold, uncomfortable things.

Most people continued to use rubber galoshes which were soft, squelchy, cold, uncomfortable things worn on top of their leather boots or shoes.

I only ever wore them in slushy conditions, preferring to stick with my well-dubbined leather boots. Instead of dubbin, most farmworkers used creesh, the lump of fat from the inside of a hen. When rubbed liberally on leather it made a first-class water repellent.

Farm and other workers wore heavy leather boots with tackets, or segs, that had to be replaced every three weeks or so. Either short leather leggings or canvas puttees went over the top of boots, and both garments needed constant brushing and scraping to prevent a build up of muck.

During World War II the local agricultural committees issued permits to enable land workers to buy wellingtons. Many men, who had never previously tried them could not resist getting what other folk were getting.

One Keith farmer asked his sister to bring home a pair. Next morning, in the blackout, he pulled on his new wellies and went to the stable to sort the horses before breakfast. When he came into the kitchen, he shouted: "Far are ma beets for I'm fair crippled with this damned wellingtons." His sister burst out laughing: "Ye muckle gype, ye've got them on the wrang feet." It is always amusing to see a young bairn pull its little wellingtons onto the wrong feet. At the first attempt, all children invariably do. But it must have been funnier still to see a mature man in the same predicament.

In the 1950s, wellingtons became more pliable. Leaks and tears could be patched just like a bicycle tube. During the 60s, we used to get leaking wellies vulcanised at the tyre depot. Sometimes it worked, mostly it didn't.

Then, in 1974, green wellies came into general use. From my point of view they could not have appeared at a better time, because two years previously I had crushed my foot in a tractor accident. Even now, I can wear only soft, flexible soles and apart from a few weeks in a dry summer, the famous green wellies are my usual footwear.

During my time in Parliament in the 70s, there were two very cold winters. The corridors of Westminster were draughty places and my legs would get cold from the ankle to the calf. I used to laugh at myself, for I was missing my wellies.

It made me realise that the teachers and doctors of my young days weren't so daft when they wore spats over their boots or shoes. The spats reached up the leg almost to the calf.

It is easy to take present day things for granted, but wellies have been a tremendous boon to fishermen, miners, farmers and others who work in wet conditions. In the days before they had the benefit of wellingtons, drainers and ditchers had to endure permanently wet feet. Small wonder that they fell easy prey to rheumatics, pneumonia and other ills.

One Irish drainer, working in the Marnoch area, was worried that his wet boots and socks would freeze overnight. His remedy was to take them off, leave them in the running water at the bottom of the drain, and go home to the bothy in clogs.

That sounds bad and bad enough, but let us put ourselves in that man's place. Think what it must have been like to reverse the procedure in the morning!

And here's me moaning about a slightly wet left foot.

Clocking-off time for broody hens!

Here's March finished and not a hen set. What is the world coming to?

I suppose there must still be some children in Scotland who are lucky enough to listen to the miracle of a young life pecking at the shell from the inside. But alas, these children are now the privileged ones because very few farmers keep poultry nowadays. Besides, many of those who do buy their stock DO (day old).

Most of the hatching is done in large commercial incubators at specialist hatcheries. The clocking hen now plays a very small part in the hatching and rearing process. Yet there was a time when many a young man took the first step to farming on his own account by setting a few broody hens.

And a lassie about to be married often received as a present a setting of eggs so that she could have a few hens of her own when she set up house with her new husband. Despite the decline in the hen's traditional role of rearing chickens, modern breeds still go broody in their second and subsequent years.

Even hens which are kept in laying cages exhibit the primeval urge to sit on eggs. They will gather all that day's laying under their wings to incubate, then fiercely resist the collector by pecking her hands.

One of the Saturday chores in our family was for us kids to be sent off in search of clocking hens. My sisters would take their bikes with a basket arrangement on the back carrier, while my brother and I went on foot, equipped with a sack on our shoulders.

We visited the near neighbours and the cyclist speired farther afield. "Hiv he ony spare clocking hens?" we'd ask, hopefully. There was no such luxury as a phone in those days.

Between us all we would gather sufficient broody hens to make the setting worthwhile. In a darkened henhouse, apple boxes would be prepared for their willing prisoners. The double apple boxes were ideal for the purpose as they were quite deep. Moist divots, large enough to cover the bottom of the boxes, were cut with a spade and placed in the boxes to form a hollow in the centre so that the eggs would not scatter to the four corners and be chilled.

Then a light covering of dry straw was shaped into a nest and the eggs carefully placed in the hollow. The hatching arrangement was completed by the addition of a light cover of sacking and a board across the top of the box to prevent the hen escaping.

Our trawl of the neighbouring farms together with the input from our own hen houses always added up to twelve, for that was the number of settings my mother liked to have at a time. Everything on a farm has its season, and I suppose looking after broody hens for twenty-eight days was long enough in any one year.

Some breeds made better mothers than others. Light Sussex and Rhode Island Red were the ideal. Hens of the lighter breeds, for instance White Leghorn or White Wyandotte, were more flighty and often went off the clock before their setting was hatched.

Most birds would sit for the twenty-one days needed to hatch out hens' eggs, but the twenty-eight days or more required for the incubation of goose eggs

Hamish tells his grand-daughters, sisters Laura (7), Claire (5) and Valerie Watt (2), about the arrival of Easter chicks.

involved a long, sair sit. And perching on top of four big eggs must have been a gey sentence for all but the laziest of hens.

Normal settings were thirteen hens' eggs, ten duck eggs, six turkey eggs and four goose eggs. These would be replicated three times to fill our complement of twelve nests.

If the hen was fully broody she would quickly settle down on a nest of her choice and peck away any feathered intruder that tried to usurp her. The hens were granted a short break twice daily to get food and water, and also to let the eggs cool down a little.

Most clockers ate very little, especially for the first fortnight. Provided they were allowed off to feed in shifts of four, there was very little poaching or breaking of eggs by careless feet.

About the fourteenth day, it was time for the exciting job of candling the eggs to see if they were fertile. With a simple tube device we would shine a torch through each egg. Those that showed up clear were discarded as infertile, while the dark ones were fertile and likely to hatch. Candles would have been used for this job in earlier times.

From that day on the eggs were lightly sprinkled with water to prevent the shell becoming too brittle and the membrane too tough. After seventeen days or so, we kids would have the great thrill of holding a hen egg to our ears and hearing a faint "tap, tap" as the embryo chick made a start to breaking out.

By day twenty, many of the eggs were chipped and you could see the tiny beak pecking away. Gradually, the chip would become a hole which eventually widened around the entire egg until the shell fell apart. A wet chick would then struggle from the egg by kicking its legs. Within a few hours it would have dried into a lovely, white fluffy chick which sat cheeping as its brothers and sisters pecked their way into the world.

After hatching, the chicks and their mother had to be transferred to a warm, dry coop with a wire run in front to prevent crows and other predators from making a meal of the little chicks.

Aye, the spring is a wonderful time when cows have calves, ewes have lambs, hens have chickens . . . and teachers have catkins and tadpoles.

Feathers and an old tar trick

There are lots of experts around when it comes to setting hens.

The wonderful response to my story of the broody hens and hatching chickens has shown that I am not alone in my liking for poultry.

I did not elaborate on the problems that used to arise when the sitting hen ceased to be broody before the eggs had hatched out. This sparked off a frantic hunt around neighbouring farms for a replacement clocker. Many readers have told me about their urgent attempts to save this particular crisis situation.

It was almost a point of honour among poultry-keepers to find a replacement broody hen before the eggs got too cold. There was a tolerance of only an hour or two before the hatching process stopped, leaving the unhatched chicks to die.

One lady, phoning me on other business, started by announcing she could let me have a "clocking duke". I can recall using a duke just once to help out with hatching a few hens' eggs among her own setting of duck eggs.

It worked perfectly well. Of course, I had to take the chicks away as soon as they were hatched and give them to a hen.

A large hen was capable of sheltering more than twelve chicks under her outspread wings, but if she had eighteen or more, there was great pressure for wing cover and heat. It used to be funny to see a small chick popping out from under a wing, then running round behind the hen to burrow under again.

The number of eggs per sitting that I quoted was correct for a sitting hen; but obviously a duck, turkey or goose that set itself, sat on many more eggs.

My mother used to be fairly successful in persuading the geese to lay in the roomy nest boxes at ground level in the goose house, and we let them hatch their brood there.

One lady reader reminds me that hens can turn their own eggs but that geese eggs have to be turned daily. Until I read her letter, I had forgotten how expertly a goose insulates her own nest with down from her breast. When the broody bird comes off the nest she carefully covers the eggs over with the down.

It was a great thrill to put your hand carefully into the nest and turn the warm eggs bottom to top. You had actually to search the large nest to make sure you hadn't missed any. I seem to recall that ten-twelve was a common clutch for geese. If there was a broody hen available to take four, we reduced the clutch to ten.

As kids, our biggest snag with geese was the fear of being pecked by the ill-tempered brutes as they fiercely guarded the nest. In addition, we never found it easy to be certain of fertile eggs. Whereas it is simple to tell cocks from hens, drakes from ducks, bubbly jocks from turkey hens, the task of telling ganders from geese is extremely difficult.

Only an expert who knows how to handle the geese and expose the sexual organs can do the job properly. Swapping geese for ganders with a neighbour was common practice, but on more than one occasion we ended up with all geese and no ganders.

It wasn't surprising that many farmers' wives preferred to buy day-old stock from the specialist hatcheries. These specialists purchased the eggs from poultry breeders and hatched them in controlled-temperature incubators. The great advantage about geese is that they are very easy to rear. Once they reach the three-week-old stage and are off the heat, they are well "roaded" and need little attention other than an evening feed.

Having fed on grass and weeds throughout the summer and autumn, six weeks of grain fattening sees them ready for the Christmas table. Nowadays, geese are in great demand as an alternative to turkey.

At Thainstone last year I saw them selling at £14 apiece. Since six geese will eat as much grass as sheep, maybe some of us should diversify into geese farming. The same dogs could easily adapt to the job of herding them.

In olden days, geese were driven to market, not carried. From Norfolk, gaggles would be herded to Smithfield in London in time for the Christmas fairs. To prevent them "going cripple" on the long journey, the birds were made to walk over molten tar several days before they set off. The idea was that a layer of tar over the feet would serve the same purpose as shoe leather.

In the American state of Virginia, I read of mixed herds (or should it be flocks?) of pigs, turkeys and geese being driven two hundred and eighty miles to South Carolina in the autumn. That must have been some pantomime, what with the turkeys needing to roost at night, the pigs needing a dry bed and the geese a wet one. The first twenty-four hours of the drove must have been sheer hell.

On such a trek, the chuckwagon carried food for more than humans. Modern transport has taken much of the romance out of rural life. I think I would have liked fine to be a drover/dealer back in those days.

Out of all the poultry we kept, my own special favourites were the ducks. The Khaki Campbells were exceptionally prolific layers and needed very little attention.

For ages, I had one small coop with six ducks. Apart from the dead of winter, they would produce six eggs every day for six days, and on the seventh day they would have seven eggs.

Incidentally, duck eggs are quite the best for baking because the albumen (the white) retains more air than a hen's egg and makes sponges and cakes lighter.

The big Aylesbury ducks were the best money spinners. They grew quickly, and a good batch weighed in at eight pound each when sixteen weeks old.

But there's aye a something. If the weather was cold and wet, the ducks were prone to rheumatism. Just like Charlie Allan, they would hirple about. Then they ceased to thrive.

Egg-traordinary time of year

I am just about falling over pheasants.

Most days I see at least four of them as I go about the farm steading feeding the animals. One particularly cheeky young cock is bound to fall victim either to a tractor wheel or to the cats.

Strangely, the cats don't seem to mind him, although I have seen several within ten feet of the bird. He wanders around on his own; and if he ventures anywhere near the many hen pheasants nesting close by, he is quickly driven off by another, much bigger, cock pheasant.

This mature bird is a real beauty. He has exceptionally long tail feathers and a wide white band completely encircles his neck. The young one, by contrast, has only a patch of white on the front of his neck.

Easter time is the season when birds and poultry lay profusely. My father used to say that any old feather duster will lay at Easter, but that it takes a good hen to lay at Christmas.

At this time of year there is a veritable glut of all varieties of eggs. I suppose that is the basic reason why some of our ancestors developed the seasonal habit of rolling eggs. I know about the religious connotations, but we won't go into that here. Suffice it to say that Easter is a festival of fun after a long, dreich winter.

It used to be great to get out of the heavy winter jersey and into a light shirt. After a long season trudging on in weighty winter boots, there was an exhilarating sense of liberation and excitement in slipping into sandshoes and setting off up the hill behind the farm. Climb to the bare patches near the very top and you could find seagull eggs by the hundred – often four to a nest.

Usually the weather is warm around Easter, unless it coincides with the "teuchats' storm", as it has done this year. The birds seem to be able to delay laying their eggs until the weather settles.

I was heavy rolling this week to get rid of the mole heaps. There were lots of peasies, oystercatchers and larks around, but no sign of eggs so far.

When horses did most of the spring work on the farms it was quite usual for the men to lift the first laying of peasies' eggs and boil them. For its size, the lapwing produces a really big egg, somewhere between pullets' egg size and mature hen size – or Grade II, as they are now known. Incidentally, Grade III eggs were being sold at Thainstone Market last Thursday at 50p for a thirty-egg tray.

I don't suppose there is such a thing as a pickling jar in the countryside nowadays. But when I was a kid the seasonal fall in the price of eggs was the signal to bring out these huge jars or urns and prepare them with fresh waterglass ready to hold ten or twenty dozen of the cheap eggs.

It was important to ensure that only naturally clean eggs were preserved. Any that had been cleaned or scrubbed were likely to absorb some of the liquid through the opened pores. The eggs kept perfectly and were used for cooking and baking throughout the rest of the year.

Easter was also the time for the "infirmary eggs". Rural schools encouraged the pupils to bring along half-a-dozen, a dozen, or preferably more eggs. I well remember that in 1940 the Keith schools exceeded their target of four hundred and forty dozen. The collection was organised by the teachers and then taken by carrier to Aberdeen Royal Infirmary where the eggs were pickled for later use.

It was no easy matter for a "hallyracket" schoolboy to get the whole dozen safely to school, on a pushbike, down a rough farm road. And of course there were no corrugated paper eggs trays and no cardboard or polystyrene containers in those days. Each egg had to be carefully wrapped in newspaper and just as carefully placed in a string bag or similar container. I can recall that it was a sair tyauve having to cycle slowly with the fragile load – and still try to get to school on time.

Nowadays, folk just grumble at how costly it is to run the National Health Service. Ye dinna ken ye're living.

And on that theme, I'd like to tell you of an incident that happened while I was in Parliament in the 70s.

As MP, I used to do a lot of lobbying on behalf of the fishing industry. For technical details and impartial advice, I could always call on Alex, who worked at the Torry Research Institute. Alex sometimes visited London in the course of his work, and on one of these occasions I was delighted to be able to invite him to dinner at the House of Commons.

We newsed away merrily over a pre-dinner drink, then progressed to the dining-room where we were duly handed a menu each. Alex gave a gasp, went white as a sheet, and looked as if he had seen a ghost. I though he had taken some kind of seizure and repeatedly asked if he was ill. "No, no. I'm all right," he kept reassuring me. Finally, over the soup course, he started to explain.

"I was brought up in Torry, the only child of very poor but devoted parents. My father was disabled and couldn't work, but he struggled to do his garden. He used to grow spinach and we ate the stuff all summer. Every spring, I was sent with the other kids in the street to the Bay of Nigg to collect seagulls' eggs. In Torry, only the poor people ate these. Anyway, my tea regularly consisted of poached seagulls' eggs on spinach, and eventually I grew heartily sick of the dish.

"Now I sit down to dinner here in the House of Commons, and what is the dearest item on the menu? For £2 extra, I can have the chef's special – poached seagull eggs on a bed of spinach!"

There's food for thought for all of us in that episode.

Gowk's corn deadline beaten

It is a good job the weather has cleared up and the land is at last drying out. Otherwise, I would have been heading for the most dreadful indignity that can befall any farmer – the necessity to plant "gowk's corn".

That's the name that has traditionally been given to barley sown in May. It has always been reckoned that crops sown in May give a poor yield and I don't suppose things have changed since the term gowk's corn was invented.

What really annoys me is that we started off in good time and got the first few fields sown in late March. The experts tell you that the ideal day to sow in March 15.

After that date, the potential yield drops by one bushel a day. From March 15 to May 1 is thirty-seven days. If we call it forty days, then we are liable to lose forty bushels, which is five quarters. Each quarter of oats weights $1^1/_2$ cwt, so we are talking about a likely loss in the region of 8 cwt. Now that could make the difference between a profitable crop and a loss-making one.

It is usually reckoned that the late crops produce more straw and less grain. Target yields are easy to set but very difficult to achieve because weather can disrupt the sowing date, the time for applying extra fertiliser and the time for spraying the weeds or mildew in the crop.

I may be girning a bit, but really I count myself lucky compared with those who farmed before me. Let's remember the doggerel about the kind of yield that our forefathers could expect:

Ane tae saw and ane tae maw,
And ane tae pey the laird witha.

To translate – the farmer looked to achieve only a threefold increase in his crop.

From each seed sown he expected to get one seed to sow next year's crop. One seed to "maw", that is, to feed himself, his family, his workers, and – most importantly – his horses. Then he needed a third seed to pay the rent.

Late-sown crops are very prone to weed growth. With early sowing, the grain gets well established and can smother the weeds which germinate later.

Because the early crops are often the cleanest, they sometimes need no spraying to eliminate weed competition. I well remember crops of oats before the days of sprays. They could be a mass of chickweed, speedwell, day nettles, thistles and fat hen.

All these, and many more, competed with the oat crop and often smothered it out. Add to that the damage inflicted by rabbits and you could have an almost total crop failure.

I clearly recollect how awful it was to stook sheaves full of thistles on a wet day. After a full morning's handling of wet sheaves your hands got soft.

Then you would pick up a sheaf full of thistle. If these were dry they went straight into your hands and fingers and became embedded. Try as you might to get them out, some would be too far in to remove except with a needle – and you didn't carry one of those in the harvest park.

Have you ever tried to milk cows with your hands full of thistles? Take it from me, it is the nearest thing to purgatory that I ever hope to get.

A reader from Speyside, Mrs Nan Fettes, has asked me if I could tell her what kind of weed a "gweel" was. She found the reference in this old rhyme:

The three worst things that Moray ere saw
Were the Gordons, the gweel, and the auld hoodie craw.

How far back that rhyme goes I cannot be sure, but in the tenth book I tried I discovered that gweel was the local name for the corn marigold. They used to grow everywhere in the early 30s.

Strong stemmed, they tasted so bitter that no animal would eat them, even among straw. Sour or acid soil was their breeding ground and they virtually disappeared after the lime subsidy was introduced in the late 30s.

Anyway, modern sprays would keep such weeds under control, although doubtless we will soon see their reappearance in the land that is under set aside.

I'm grateful to Mrs Fettes for having set me off on that search because I came across many more items of interest. For example, farmers in Moray were not free to grind their grain where they chose, but had to patronise a meal mill of the landlord's choosing.

They were also duty bound to sell all grain through this one merchant and had to deliver the sold crop to the nearest port on a specified day. As early as the 16th century and probably long before that, there was a thriving trade in malt shipments to Norway.

Doubtless the many malting companies operating in Moray still sell malt to Norway. They certainly sell to countries as far away as Nigeria and to many places in between. So, compared to our predecessors there is not a lot coming over us.

That's the rain on again. I doot it's gaun tae to be a drabbly year. But at least I'm saved from gowk's corn.

Fishy tales from the past

With a surname like mine I must have come from Gamrie.

Although I have never bothered to trace my pedigree, I understand that some of my forbears hailed from Lossiemouth.

Anyway, Watt is a Gamrie/Macduff name, and with my liking for the sea and things fishing I am content to claim connection. Although nowadays there is little comings and goings between fishing and farming, this was not always the case.

Fishing boats are plenished from the local grocery store with enough food supplies to last the trip. And as fishing has been, in the main, very profitable over the past twenty years, no skipper has seen the need to query the cost of feeding his crew.

I have been to sea in different fishing vessels seven times in all and on each occasion the crew and I have fed exceptionally well. In the hard times prior to World War II, adequate, nutritious meals were by no means the general rule. Some years the boats ended the fishing season deeper in debt than when they began and this made it imperative to feed the crew as cheaply as possible.

Fishwives and fish cadgers bought or bartered for food from the farms and the farmers' wives in turn bought their fish. For every dozen herring purchased, you got thirteen.

I can well remember two fishwives from Lossiemouth selling speldings to my mother on a Saturday in exchange for butter, cheese or duck eggs. A delicacy they were especially fond of was freshly-made crowdie.

On completion of their dealing in the kitchen, the two women would hoist their heavy creels onto their backs and take to the road, contentedly enjoying an oatcake quarter heaped with crowdie.

I can also remember the sheer delight expressed by my mother's summer visitors at breakfast next morning when they had the speldings and an egg poached in milk.

Although they did wear heavy oilskin coats in really wet weather, these women must have had many a soaking when caught in a sudden shower with only their black knitted shawls for protection.

Not all fish cadgers were from the coast. A kindly old man by the name of Sandy Gracie lived in a very humble dwelling on a tiny croft at the back of the hill about two miles from our farm near Keith. We were his final customer before he tackled the rough road home and he needed a sheaf of corn for his white Sheltie.

He lived alone, so he often found time to stay for a boiled egg and tea, with an oatcake. His pony was too small to pull the cairtie with its two fish boxes and its owner on the rough tracks up the hill. Sandy simply had to walk alongside for most of the way.

Eager to refresh my memory about Sandy Gracie, I phoned my three sisters, all of whom are older than myself. Only the eldest could recall the name and none of them could actually remember the old man. Faced with this blank response, I was beginning to think I had imagined this particular character and his circumstances. I was, therefore, more than pleased to be speaking at Huntly mart to an 83-year-old retired farmer, who immediately recalled the fishman with his wee cairtie and his "fite Shelt". He could even remember a brown shelt before the white one.

My informant reckons that Sandy must have had his fish consigned daily from Buckie up the old Highland Line to Keith Station. There would have been a once-weekly trip to Buckie for a square-up.

Back in the last century, the fisherman were much more dependent on the farmers, because their basic diet consisted of milk, kail turnips, fish and potatoes. It would seem that "Cullen Skink" is of very ancient origin. Barley meal cakes were the staple bread, oatmeal was little heard of and oatcakes were considered a luxury.

To the farmers, they sold herrings, haddocks, dried cod and dogfish, the last being considered a great delicacy. Nowadays, hardly anybody in this neck of the woods eats dogfish. We send them away to England and other such foreign parts.

I recently read in an old history of the Buckie district that in addition to selling fish, the 19th-century fishmen used to cadge "skate oil" – widely regarded as the best for oil lamps.

This would have been before the days of Paraffin Young and his greatly advanced kerosene lamps. And that was before the Tilley lamp, the gas lamp and the electric light. We have come a long way in a remarkably short time.

In the same book I was intrigued to discover that in 1826 the first iron plough in the district was brought to Buckie by the Laird of Cluny. Pulled by four oxen, it broke in an area of ground to the south of Buckie that had previously been poor moorland covered in whins.

The clearly-described areas are today the six finest fields on my farm. Hardly a drain has been required in the whole ninety acres. It is beautiful, free-draining soil that will neither "drucht nor droon". I always assumed that it had been arable land for much longer than one hundred and sixty-six years.

It has been my pleasure and privilege to have farmed that land for the past twenty years. the soil was in great heart when I bought it, so some excellent farmers must have worked it before I saw it.

Apart from buying some dung for their gardens, fishermen now have no direct selling or bartering links with farmers. Maybe it's time to rectify that.

I feel sure that there must be some deep freezes easily capable of holding one of my surplus lambs. and for my part, I eat fish at least twice a week – more in the herring season.

Days of the Rothiebrisbane bonnets . . .

I see the swallows are back, the grass is growing and the dandelions are ready for the young boys' rabbits.

"But the spring is nae really in till the lads wi the nerra breeks tak the road." These used to be words of a well-known cattle dealer, Frank Smythe.

The lads he was referring to were the "staiggers", or stallion grooms, who travelled many miles leading their huge Clydesdale stallions from farm to farm.

Adhering as best they could to a strict itinerary, their rounds took them to the same farm every twenty-one days in their endeavour to mate their stallions with as many mares as possible in the spring and summer season.

The replacement of working farm horses by tractors in the years following World War II led to the total demise of the travelling stallions. And in any case, with so much heavy traffic on our roads it would no longer be safe to lead such temperamental, powerful brutes around the countryside.

The introduction of horseboxes and livestock trailers has also helped to bring about a fundamental change. Nowadays, the owner of a mare requiring the services of a stallion can take the female to the male, instead of the other way round.

The stallions were big, magnificent beasts, superbly turned out. Frequent grooming kept their coats clean and shiny and the hair on their legs – the feathers – was washed at least once a day. They always looked so perfect compared to the mares, whose bodies might be sweat-stained and mud spattered from their work.

Similarly, the stallion grooms were very much smarter than the average farmworker. The staigger's suit was immaculately clean, his boots shone, and he wore a collar and tie.

I can remember being highly amused at one staigger washing his plastic white collar at the horse trough in our farm close. There was often resentment to this visiting dandy if any of the farm lasses took a shine to him.

Little boys were kept away from the stable on stallion days, but we could watch from the safety of the farm loft. There was no need for stories of birds and bees for us lads.

As well as the "nerra breeks", most staiggers wore long jackets with high-cut shoulders sculpted like the Deveron brig, it was said. Some of them favoured ordinary cloth caps, but most wore another badge of their trade, the Rothiebrisbane bonnet.

They were very similar to the Kilmarnock bonnets worn farther south, but they lacked the wire. Generally, the Rothiebrisbane bonnets came in varying shades of blue, with a diced headband and toorie of a different colour. Stallion grooms can still be seen wearing this distinctive headgear at shows such as the Winter Fair at Ingliston.

The stallions invariably carried impressive names denoting strength and power. Masterstroke, Hiawatha, Footprint, Prince of Wales were some examples. These were prefixed by the name of the farm where the animal was bred, producing titles like Danure Footprint, Doura Masterstroke and so on. Some stallions were booked by local horse-breeding societies to stand a season in their district, and the owner

of the horse would have been paid a premium. But as well as these club horses, as they were known, there were always poachers who took pot luck in cadging for business. A successful poacher could obtain close on one hundred mares in the season, thus earning good money for the stallion master and the groom.

This spring I was honoured to be invited as guest speaker by Nairnshire Agricultural Society. My genial host, the society president, Mr James McBain, was kind enough to lend me two volumes of the transactions of the society to enable me to undertake some background research. The society will be celebrating its 200th birthday in seven years, so there must be a wealth of material in its earlier volumes.

The records given to me dated back to 1908 and I was fascinated to discover the distinguised roll-call of fairly recent speakers. Here were men like Arthur Wannop, Fraser Darling, Watt Taylor and many other giants of the farming world who have left their mark on our industry.

Throughout the volumes, running parallel to the transactions of the society, were reports of the meetings of the horse-breeding committee. The annals clearly revealed that Nairnshire engaged the finest stallions available in Scotland. The excellence of Nairnshire livestock would seem to have been mirrored in the past by the outstanding quality of the horses bred there.

Something that really amused me was the note in each annual report which stated: "The next item on the agenda being the horse-breeding report, the ladies of the society left the meeting." What prudes our forefathers must have been to pretend that ladies knew nothing about procreation.

Things have changed to such an extent that at the pony studs now the vast majority of stallion grooms are ladies. Very efficient they are, I may say. And coincidentally they, too, wear "nerra breeks" – either jeans or jodphurs.

All this is reminding me of the story about the farmer who turned up at the local stud farm and found only the daughter at home. He asked if her father would be long in coming back. "He won't be back until evening, Mr Brown," said the girl, "but if it's the boar you are needing, I can easily handle him and the fee is £1." "No, I'd better see your father," was the reply.

"Oh, if it is the bull you're needing I can easily handle him and the fee is £2."
"No, I'd better see your father," repeated Mr Brown. "Well, if it's the stallion you're needing I can easily handle him and the fee is £5." "No, it isn't any of these I'm needing, Mary," said Mr Brown. "But as you will find out soon enough, I might as well tell you. Your brother Davie has got my lassie into trouble."

"Oh, in that case you'll need to see my father, then," said Mary, "because I don't know what we charge for Davie."

Now. Would that story belong to the present or the past?

When farmworkers faced a fee-for-all . . .

"Are ye flitting or are ye biding?" This is May, the traditional month for moving on. Both farmers and farmworkers regarded Whitsunday (May 28) as the most important day of the year. The "Mey term" was the main date for farmers to take a new tenancy or to relinquish the tenancy of the farm they were on. They would either retire, or take what they hoped would be a better place.

Prior to the passing of the 1948 Agricultural Act, there was much greater mobility among farmers than is now the case. The act provided the security of tenure which gave the tenant farmer the opportunity to improve his farm, and to be compensated for so doing. For the majority of farmers, these changes spelt the end of the constant search for a bigger, better place. And anyway, the number of farms coming available for let has declined dramatically.

But it was to the farmworker that Whitsunday really belonged. On that day, he was free to leave the terrible place he'd had to endure for the past six months; and surely any new place would be better than yon. Some were fortunate to land at a more congenial farm. Some found that they were out of the frying pan and into the fire.

Many farm servants must have found it trying to live cheek by jowl with other men in a small bothy for six months on end, and any change would have been welcome. If a lad was lucky he could get a step-up from orraman to third horseman, and thence to second horseman. The second horseman was usually entrusted with the job of breaking in the young colts, and that was a challenge to be looked forward to.

Wages were low and the work was hard. The farmers often cared more for their horses than they did for their men. Men could be replaced at no cost. There were always plenty of chiels looking for a fee, and a host of willing young boys keen to get started in farm work. The fortunate few would begin an apprenticeship when they were sixteen. Two years of farm life stood them in good stead with a prospective employer.

Usually when a lad, fresh from school, was looking for a fee, his father would accompany him to the feeing market. The feeing markets were held in rural towns in the first two weeks of May; and in the hungry 30s, many a lad had to attend several before he found himself a place.

I can recall hearing about one young lad who found himself in the following predicament. He was attending Huntly feeing market, and the father told him to hold out for £14 for the six months. Before long father met in with some cronies and adjourned to the nearest pub, leaving his son to fend for himself. Eventually, the lad was approached by a farmer. "You're a strong-looking lad. Are you looking for a fee?" "Aye," said the boy, "and I'm well accustomed to farm work. I can pu' neeps and sort nowt. And I've already done a hairst". "Well," said the farmer, "it sounds as if you might suit me. I'll give you £15 for your six months." "Oh! in that case I canna come tae ye," said the loon, "because my father said I had to get £14 and its £14 I maun get."

My father never liked feeing markets and much preferred to hire his staff privately beforehand. However, I remember than on more than one occasion a lad decided to leave at the last minute. The grieve would then be sent to the market to engage a likely lad – and invariably he got 'foo'.

It seemed to me that in the late 30s the recruiting sergeants had the best job on the feeing market days as they sought to recruit any lad who didn't immediately get a fee. Often, they took advantage of a young boy who had taken more drams than he could handle. Very few farmworkers had money to spend on drink in those days because they were paid only at the end of their six months stint. Most tried hard not to seek a sub (that is, part payment between the terms of Whitsunday and Martimas – November 28).

When war broke out in 1939, the Government imposed a standstill order on all farmworkers. this was bitterly resented to begin with, but opposition soon died down as both farmers and worker realised that there was a better way to conduct affairs than to have men standing on a street corner bargaining their labour with no security of tenure on either side. Certainly, by the time freedom of movement was restored at the end of the war, nobody wanted to return to the bad old days of taking pot luck.

The taking and giving of references became commonplace. Once during the 60s, I advertised in the *Press and Journal* for a grieve, and one of the applicants was a George Barclay. He gave as referee Bob Anderson, of Aucharnie, Forgue – a farmer I knew well. Now, Bob was a high Tory of the old school and many a friendly but heated argument I had with him.

"If your needing a good, reliable man who can turn his hand to anything, George Barclay is your man. But he is a bit of a socialist, mind," Bob told me. "How do you mean a socialist?" I asked. "Well, he lived and worked on an out-farm of mine, and we kept in touch by phone. He would ring me up of an evening and say: 'Hello, Is that you Bob? This is Mr Barclay here'."

I daresay John Major, with his calls for a classless society, would have been proud of George today. Maybe even Toryism, like time, moves on.

Step back in time on Borders trip

The spring work was finished – even the stones had been gathered from the barley fields yet again. This year we have been using a different plough and it seems to have brought a greater number of big stones to the surface.

To avoid breakages of machinery it is essential to remove all the stones bigger than two fists. The smaller ones will then get pushed under the surface with a heavy roller.

Stone gathering is a job that always takes longer than you think and it is only when the tractor trailer wheels leave deep tracks that you realise there are three or four tons on board. Ten trailer loads and we were finished.

It seemed to me that a wee break was called for – just to see how the other half of the country was faring. I had heard that the West had experienced a particularly wet spring. The saying that the world is ill divided certainly holds true in Scotland. The West gets too much rain, while here in the East we are often crying out for a shower.

There seems little doubt that the extra tree cover in the West is encouraging clouds to deposit their rain there. As a consequence, the East is becoming something of a rain shadow.

Anyway, with the dairy cows now out at grass, I decided to take a long weekend off. And as if I needed an excuse to enjoy a few days in the Borders, I saw an advert for the dispersal sale of a small herd of dairy cows down there.

Thankfully, the dry weather had reached the South-west three days before the sale, and the dubs were beginning to dry up. But the poached pastures were clear evidence that it had indeed been a late, wet spring. My story about the gowk's corn would not be appreciated in that area because a lot of ploughed land hasn't yet been sown. Farmers to whom I spoke claimed it was the latest sowing they had ever known. Many doubted the economics of sowing so late, but what else could they do?

Arriving at the farm where the sale was to take place I took one step into the dairy byre and was transported back forty-five years. There stood the cows, tied by their necks in single byres. In daily use were the type of bucket machines we replaced forty years ago with pipeline milking. This latter method was, in its turn, superseded twenty years ago by parlour milking. On this Borders farm, the milk was carried in pails across the close to the dairy, lifted into a water cooler and later transferred to the refrigerated bulk milk tank. I now realise why there are twenty-seven electric motors around our farm.

No concession had been made to mechanical mucking, either. There was still total dependence on the old graip and barrow. I say graip, but a shovel would have been the better tool because there was very little straw among the muck. The cows themselves were fit but not fat. A local man at the ringside told me that the outgoing farmer had always bought straw from him, but apparently never quite enough.

After settling the bill with the auction company and phoning my floater in Portsoy to let him know that there were twenty-two cattle ready for transportation from Beattock to Buckie, I was free for the rest of the weekend.

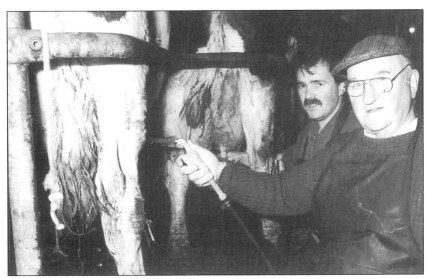

In his own more modern milking unit, Hamish Watt with his son, Michael

The farm had been easy enough to find, although tucked deep into the rolling Border hills. Not two roofs of the steading ran in the same direction, and the whole place would have made an ideal setting for an episode of *All Creatures Great and Small*.

The traditional South-west farmhouse, with the dairy hard by, was well whitewashed, but the lady of the house told me it was cold and damp in cold and damp weather – which is often. The farm had been in her husband's family for generations, with nephew taking over from uncle when already in middle-age. There had been no young blood around for a very long time, and the place showed it.

When the sale was over I was invited to join the family, their neighbours and helpers at a table spread with delicious home-baking. The bowl of steaming hot soup was most acceptable after three hours of standing while implements, sheep and cattle were sold. When the sun went down the wind was still biting. Over the tea I learned a lot about the animals I'd bought from the kindly farmer. He was obviously fond of his livestock and will undoubtedly miss them in his retirement.

Business done, I resumed my holiday with a lovely drive along a narrow valley from Moffat to Selkirk via the Grey Mare's Tail and St Mary's Loch. The introduction of the four-wheeled, all terrain vehicle ATV has proved a tremendous boon in the steep Borders hills. A shepherd can now get round his sheep easily and often, whereas in the past men and boys were exhausted before they started work by the steep climb from the farm steading at the bottom of the valley to the open pasture at the top.

The South Country cheviots have lambed well this year, despite the wet weather. Blackface lambs are still small and lovely, with their Persil-white coats and shiny black faces not yet dirtied by a summer storm.

Some sheep farms have been planted with trees, but only a proportion of these are growing well. The forests on the north-facing slopes are very patchy and some appear "stuck". Obviously, sections of the land are unsuitable for trees and would be better left under sheep.

As I drove mile after mile along that road I marvelled at the excellent state of the dry-stone dykes. I marvelled even more at the husbandry of the men who had built them so many centuries ago. These high dykes have stood the test of time, providing shelter for the sheep in all weathers. I thought of the millions of tons of stones that had been collected from the fields and carefully built into these permanent structures. My efforts in collecting forty tons from the barley fields are paltry by comparison. My stones were simply flattened to fill a hole. I can fully appreciate the efforts of these early Border men who had no mechanical aids to help them.

It seems wrong to abandon the work of our forefathers. It would make sense that we, as a nation, should have proper land-use planning to preserve such a heritage. There may again come a day when we need the produce of these Border hills.

Later, reaching the kindlier land of East Lothian, I saw several flocks being paddock-grazed on heavily fertilised grassland. I couldn't but compare the lot of these closely-packed sheep with that of their neighbours on the open hills. If I were a sheep, I know the life I would prefer.

As I said, a few days away from home does you good. It helps to put things into perspective.

Gowk's corn – it just didn't add up!

I used to think I was good at arithmetic and mental arithmetic was one of my favourite subjects in the higher classes at primary school.

But the other week I made a right hash of calculating the potential loss of the crop in my article on "gowk's corn".

To begin with, I miscounted the number of days from the ideal sowing date of March 15 to the dreaded May 1 – gowk's corn day. Then, by carelessly mixing up quarters with half quarters, I compounded the error. I'm sorry to say I'll have to accept nothing out of 10 for that effort.

The flood of letters pointing out my mistakes has been so great that I will be unable to reply to them individually. But I do enjoy receiving readers' comments – even when I'm being ticked off.

It is not as if I had any excuse for my mistake, as I've had my share of the corn end at a threshing mill. The grain was run into strong jute sacks that held a half-quarter. If oats were being threshed, there were three fifty-sixers on the besemer (weighing machine); and if we were threshing barley there were the four weights, that is, 2 cwt. In some places the sacks had to be carried up a stair to a loft for storage and that was sair work, indeed.

There used to be a nationwide sack hire service with depots dotted throughout the countryside. Sacks could be drawn say in Elgin and the purchaser of the grain might return them empty to a store in Montrose. If the grain was being exported, each sack had to be emptied into the hold of the ship.

Nowadays, all grain in handled in bulk by augurs or travelling belts and sacks are a thing of the past. This change has been a blessing to farmers, but, of course, the demise of the sack played merry hell with the jute trade. It is also great that the grain is now measured by weight – cwt and tonnes.

There must be a generation that has grown up never having seen a blue school jotter with all the tables printed at the back. Some of the terms referred to there were obsolete even when I was a bairn. I never knew what a peck was, although I did know about bushels and quarters.

When it came to measuring, I never used perches or roods. These had gone out of general use by the time I was at school in the 30s and early 40s. I only ever grappled with square yards and acres. Now, of course, our units of measurement are confined to square metres and hectares.

In measuring weight there used to be grammes, ounces, pounds, stones, hundredweights and tons. The Common Market may have done us little good, but at least it forced us into decimalisation and ended forever the kind of nightmare sums we scholars had to work out.

How many readers could now calculate the cost of 3 cwt, 5 st, 11 lb, 3 oz of potatoes at $5^1/_2$d (fivepence ha'penny) a stone? And do you know something – I'm not even going to try. I might get it wrong.

I am not, however, prepared to eat humble pie regarding my story about the laddie at the feeing market holding out for £14 for his six months' work. Several readers have written to tell me that the boys never got as much as that.

Those who keep diaries may be able to prove me wrong, but if my memory serves me right, that kind of money was being offered in 1939. In that year, a lad of eighteen was fee-ed to our farm at the May term for £18 for his half year to drive (ca) the orra horse.

Incidentally, our "orra" horse was anything but orra. She was a well set up, good looking black Cydesdale mare called Queen. She frequently bred good foals, mostly male, that fetched high prices when they were four years old. Orra horses were so called because they were not one of a pair.

On the other hand, orramen or orra loons had no horses at all. They carried out all the orra work, which was anything and everything other than driving a pair of horses.

Anyway, this lad Geordie had been on the farm only two months when he was invited to his sister's wedding. Up until then he had never owned a suit, but it was essential that he wear one at the wedding because he was to be an usher. He agonised for days before plucking up courage to ask the grieve to approach my father for the sub of £1.

Farmers were under no obligation to pay any of the agreed wage until the term day at the end of the six month engagement. And worse than that, if a man left the farm during the six months and thus broke his contract, he wasn't even entitled to receive the money he had already worked for.

I was speaking to Willie Low from Torphins about these far-off days and he knew of one instance where a young fellow with a fiery temper left his farms before the term twice on the run. For fifteen months on end he received no cash whatever, only his keep.

My father never held with these barbaric working conditions and considered them grossly unfair. I often used to hear him argue with his fellow farmers about better conditions for agricultural workers.

I think I can hear him yet when in 1940 the Wages Board stipulated that workers were to get Saturday afternoons off. Many farmers were up in arms over this apparently outrageous suggestion. They were all going to be ruined, or so they claimed. These doom merchants got no support from my father. "We will nae doot manage somehow", was his quiet rejoinder. And we did.

Well anyway, Geordie got his £1 sub no bother and set off to shop for a suit after his day's work. In those pre-war times it wasn't only farmworkers who had long hours. Drapers shops did not close until nine o'clock on Saturday nights.

Geordie's very presentable three-piece was bought in Hepworths for eighteen shillings. And that meant he had something left over to put into the pooch – he had all of two shillings to stand his hand at the wedding.

Not coorse, just ill-tricket!

I was never a good boy.

When I was young, any lad who qualified for such a title was regarded as a cissy and someone to be avoided. On the other hand, I was never a member of a gang and never in trouble with the bobbies.

Yet, I earned the enduring reputation of being a "coorse loon". Maybe it was because I occasionally rebelled against authority. This was especially true when that authority was exercised by my elder sisters, who were inclined to be bossy. The eldest, who was my senior by some six years, used to issue orders as if she were the farm gaffer and I suppose she got annoyed when I didn't carry them out.

Anyway, I had my own Saturday jobs to do without her interference. A child about a farm doesn't have to be very old to be useful. By the time I was six, I had the task of cleaning out the nests in the henhouses, using a hoe without a handle. That done, I proceeded to the cuffin shed for a bagful to re-line the nests.

It is difficult to describe what "cuffins" were. They were neighter the straw nor the chaff, but rather a mixture of both. Only the old-fashioned barn mills produced the cuffins, which fell from the shakers at a stage after the chaff. They were nice and soft and were certainly more effective than the brittle straw in helping to prevent egg breakages.

My mother was a bit inclined to hit out first and ask questions later. Perhaps that explains why I got so many clips round my bare legs with a wet dishcloth. There's one particular punishment that is still very fresh in my memory.

Like most kids reared on the early Tarzan films, it was essential for us to have a house in a tree. My brother Percy and I had quite a secure platform – well, at least six planks – sufficient, anyway, for the creating of fantasies and the dreaming of dreams.

One day I climbed down to fetch something and had just reached the foot of the tree when Percy came tumbling through the branches and hit the ground hard.

Maybe I have a warped sense of humour, but the sight of him hitting every branch on the way down highly amused me and I started laughing.

I quickly helped him to the house and my mother took one look at Percy crying and one look at me laughing. Unfortunately, she jumped to the wrong conclusion and gave me the most awful hiding on the bare legs with the wooden spoon she happened to have in her hand. I can hear and feel the whacks yet.

By the time Percy got stopped crying sufficiently to tell her it wasn't my fault, I was crying too. Fifty years ago nobody had invented the notion that smacking children was wrong. Besides, my mother had her own theory about rearing children. It was work, work and more work. To be caught reading anything other than school books was a fault and always led to more orders for extra work.

All the milk-delivery boys get up to some devilment and I was no worse than the rest. But being the milkman's son, I usually got the blame.

Still, it was fun to climb onto the roof of a low house and shin up the skew to put a slate or a divot on the chimney. We always chose a lum that was already billowing a lot of reek from a newly-lit fire. By the time the occupants had rushed to the door, we milkboys were busy dropping bottles at the house across the street. The well-known trick of using a pin, a long thread and a button to tap, tap on a livingroom window was too slow for us. We just couldn't spare enough time to do it effectively. For instant results, nothing could beat tying two adjacent front doors together with a length of string and then ringing the bells. If the string was the right length, the see-saw movement of the doors was really hilarious to watch. But there was a snag: the householders could usually see who the culprits were.

I will admit that we were very cruel when it came to giving nicknames. One customer used to come to the door and call to her son: "Come and get yer Cremola, Jim!" The lad was forever after known as Cremola Jim.

At another house we would be delivering the milk just as the daughter was leaving to go out for the evening. As we filled the jug, her mother would call: "Mind – ten o'clock, Jean". We milk lads christened the girl ten o'clock Jean and, sadly for the poor lass, the name stuck.

Now, I will admit there was one time we were gey ill-trickit. Old Doddy liked a dram and he took quite a few as he sold early tatties round the town. His last customer used to give him tea to help sober him up for the twelve mile journey home. His old horse, Dolly, stood motionless outside the house; and one Saturday we led her slowly and quietly across the street to the Mills of Keith.

The mills had a heavy, ornate wrought-iron gate which we opened. We unharnessed the pony from the shafts and trundled the cart to the inside of the gate, then turned it around and pushed the shafts through the bars. Then we reharnessed the mare and sat down to wait and watch on a dyke farther along the street.

When Doddy came out from his tea, there was the horse on one side of the gate and his cart on the other. "Good God, Dolly, what a predicament to get yersel intae," he shouted. "Loons, come and gie me a hand". Barely able to keep our faces straight, we quickly reversed the process. A grateful Doddy gave us both a sixpence – and to our eternal shame, we took it.

Still, I wouldn't say I was "coorse", even although my mother often professed that she was "black affrontit" by me. Mind you, about six years ago at Keith Show a sprightly, middle-aged lady approached me and asked if I was Hamish Watt.

It turned out that she had been a kitchenmaid at our farm when I was a little boy. I was, she announced, the coorsest little b★★★★★ that she had ever come across.

She went on: "I have followed your career with great interest, because I always thought it would be a criminal one".

"Oh Peg," I replied, "I remember you well and I was really fond of you". Back came the comment: "Yes, Hamish, and I was fond of you, too. But you were still the coorsest little b★★★★★".

Now, if I had been a really good boy, would Peg have taken half as much interest in my progress through life?

Fifty fly in and bring a summer message

One swallow doesn't make a summer, but will fifty do?

Most years, six to eight swallows arrive back at our farm in mid-May. I have always presumed that it is the survivors of last year's hatch which return.

These three or four pairs set about commandeering and repairing the nests occupied the previous year. Unless the summer is a poor one, they will hatch out two broods of young as a rule. Each hatch results in four or five wee faces peeping over the mud walls, calling out to be fed.

As August gives way to September, the air is filled with young birds swooping and diving, catching insects and building up their strength for the long migration to sunny Africa where they overwinter.

For several weeks before departure they congregate in the late evening on the electric wires between the buildings. There they sit against the sky with their heads above the wire and their forked tails below, looking for all the earth like clothes pegs on a washing line. It is easy to count them and between one hundred and one hundred and twenty is the common score.

Well, this year on April 29 we could observe only five swallows around the steading, and these made no attempt to build nests. Then suddenly, twelve days later, there were swallows everywhere. This time, though, they are all so busy and so restless that an accurate count has not been possible. Certainly, there are more than fifty; and nests are being constructed in places where none have been built before.

We have lots of strong iron girders supporting the wide-spanned roofs on some of our sheds. The L beams and the H beams make excellent supports for the base of the nests, and the mud the birds use seems to cling well to the slightly rough iron surface of the beams.

It has been a dry spring and summer, so the swallows are spending their time near the milking parlour door, where the water from the powerful jets of the washing pumps spills out among the earth and the muck that the cows bring in on their feet.

The combination of water and mud is greatly to their liking and all the nests have been built in record time. I often wonder if such skills are totally inherited or if there is a degree of teaching by last year's parents. Anyway, the nests are up and each contains four to six eggs.

At this time of year on beef farms all the calves are out at grass suckling their mothers. By contrast, we dairy farmers rear our calves by feeding milk from buckets and the calves mostly remain inside for the first sixteen weeks of life while they are on milk.

In warm weather, overcrowding must be avoided to prevent the spread of coughs and pneumonia. Consequently, our calves are spaced thinly in various sheds – those same sheds as the swallows are using.

Feeding and tending the calves takes only thirty minutes three times a day, but the swallows resent our intrusion into their territory. They dive in through the doorways at full tilt and often nearly collide with the human inside. They are frequently within inches of my head before they put on the brakes, change direction and swoop back out through the doorway. Outside, they twitter and chatter in great rage – furious at me for daring to hinder them in their vital work.

I've had a tedious and arm-breaking job these last few days, rogueing the wild oats from the field of winter barley. We have a tremendous crop of the six-rowed variety Manitou. It is so thick that it's difficult to walk through. The crop is about four feet, but the wild oat straws are a foot higher and easily seen.

We had sprayed to check the wild oat menace earlier in the summer, and that has resulted in a very good kill. Unfortunately, some strips have been missed and it's these I'm attempting to clean out.

One wild oat plant has very little weight, but by the time I have pulled several hundred and thrown them over my left arm the burden gets heavy. Carrying the bulky heap of rogues through the thick crop to the edge of the field is a tiring, weighty task. It certainly brings to life the observation about the straw that broke the camel's back.

At the height of the day the sun was too hot for such work, so I set to in the "forenicht". I had swallows galore for company then. You know, it is a terrible shame that we allow words such as "evening" to supplant the guid Scots' "forenicht". To "convoy" somebody is so much couthier than to "accompany". I still go out for a "traivel" rather than a walk.

It used to be standard practice in fine weather during high summer to take a forenicht traivel to a neebor's place just for a news. You would see through their beasts, admire the half-grown chickens, compare notes about the young turkeys committing suicide and generally give the affairs of the parish a fair "ca thru".

Then, after a cup of tea with a taste of the newly-made cheese and a bit of fine hame baking, your neebor would convoy you about half way home. "Seeing you past the hens' meat", my mother used to call it.

Well, the swallows convoyed me the whole two hours as they swooped and dived above the crop. The midges and countless other insects were disturbed by my walking through the barley, and the swallows took full advantage of the situation.

Already there are some small patches of the barley crop going down, especially where we had applied too much dung last autumn. A heavy shower of rain and more of it will go down – permanently. A laid crop is rarely a profitable one, particularly if it goes down early. Moreover, the laid patches encourage pigeons and crows to attack the grain at the milk stage.

On the other hand, if the weather continues dry and warm we could have early ripening and the crop would yield well. So I'm looking for a fine summer. One swallow does not make a summer, but there are fifty this year. Do you think we should read a promising message into that?

Wool fair now spins a new yarn

The year is racing on.

Here we are at mid-July already. One snag about farming is that we are always too busy on fine days to really enjoy the weather.

Anyway, the sun shone every day at silage-making, and we should have an abundance of excellent winter feed for the dairy cows. We also make a lot of hay for sheep and young cattle, but so far it has been an uphill job, with sunless days and drabbly nichts.

Regardless of the weather, the farming calendar rolls relentlessly on and the second Friday of July marks the Wool Fair at Inverness. Despite the name, the one thing you will not find at Inverness that day is wool.

Still, the two auction marts attract a huge influx of people from throughout Scotland and in particular from the Highlands. There are many trade stands selling goods relevant to the horse and pony business.

I have been unable to establish when the Wool Fair started, but there are plenty of old photographs depicting wool merchants from Scotland and the North of England sitting on benches in Inverness Station concourse. There, they were approached by the farmers or their agents from the big sheep farms in the North and West.

After the Highland Clearances the stocks of Cheviots and Cheviot crosses produced large quantities of fine quality wool, the finest in Britain for the worsted trade.

The sellers would produce a representative sample of the freshly-clipped fleeces, prices were bargained and finally agreed. The bulk supply was then transported by train to the purchasers' premises, and a fair proportion of the wool subsequently bought by the many woollen mills throughout the Highlands and the North-east. Sadly, most of these are now closed.

Over the years, trading in wool was taken over by merchants who sold sheep dip to the farmers as part of the deal. Then in the late 1940s, buying passed exclusively to the British Wool Marketing Board. The board has been the instrument for steady improvement in the quality of wool presented for sale.

It has also evened out the peaks and troughs of market prices. And it has fruitfully co-operated with its counterparts in the prime wool-producing countries of Australia, New Zealand and South Africa.

Now, though, the government seems determined to remove the stability that wool producers have enjoyed for nigh on fifty years. The wool board is shortly to lose all marketing powers, and the slump in prices will undoubtedly accelerate without its stabilising influence.

One important part of the Wool Fair day was the bargains struck between Highland flockmasters and low-ground farmers concerning the wintering of hill hoggs for the period October 1 to April 1 the following spring.

These female flock replacements could not survive on the open hill in their first winter of life. Any that did manage to make it had their growth stunted through lack of adequate pasture.

It is highly probable that the buying and selling of horses on that July Friday in Inverness pre-dates the wool fair by hundreds of years. The early horse fairs took place on the banks of the River Ness, but with the advent of the railways, the sale moved to the station yard and horses were trotted out close by the loading banks.

Now, horses and ponies are sold indoors at Hamilton's Mart and there is no opportunity for prospective buyers to see the animals in action. However, many carry a vet's certificate to prove their fitness.

My farming friends in the Highlands talk of seven hundred horses being traded in the heyday of the Wool Fair. That would have meant several train loads of horseboxes leaving Inverness Station bound for cities across Britain. The heavy horses were destined to pull wagons while lighter ponies were used for gigs and carriages.

Wherever there are horses you will find a great congregation of toffs and tinks. These two sections of society seem to share a fascination for horseflesh in all breeds, colours and sizes. This year was no exception, and the sale ring was thronged with a wide variety of humanity from throughout the country.

I only looked in for a few minutes to see the lovely creatures (I mean the horses) and was fortunate enough to witness a beautiful black and white gelding sell for £1,700.

The Wool Fair was traditionally the sale where Highland estates bought Highland garrons for working on the shooting moors. Ponies that were trained to carrying panniers were at a premium, and those guaranteed to carry deer carcases were eagerly sought after. Now, the tracked and four-wheeled vehicles have made the garrons redundant on moor and hill, and reduced their role to pony trekking.

My first involvement with the Wool Fair dates from the 1950s when I sold quiet cows for hand-milking to the Highland crofters. At that time, Jersey cows were bought by shooting estates to supply the guests with fresh, creamy milk.

This, too, has changed. Supplies are procured twice weekly from the local village shop or the nearest supermarket, since milk has a wonderfully long shelf life nowadays and daily supplies are not necessary.

There used to be a magnificent display of dairy cattle forward at the Wool Fair when upwards of three hundred, including bulling heifers, would be traded.

Recently, I was thrilled to have a phone call about one of my stories from Murdo Munro of Dallas. Now in his mid-eighties, Murdo used to present around twenty beautifully turned out dairy shorthorn heifers each July, and often gained top prices. Last week, there were less than twenty dairy cattle forward, but the numbers of beef cows and calves are gradually increasing.

Times are changing and I'll just have to change with them. Maybe I'll hold back some of my spring-calving beef heifers until July, so that I can continue to have an excuse to pay my annual visit to the Wool Fair.

I wouldn't like to be merely a spectator and I can never bring myself to get involved in buying and selling ponies. I have never pretended to be a toff and there isn't enough of the tink in me. Or so my political opponents used to say.

Shep, my shagg-dog story

My dog is an orra working brute. All in all, he is a very orra dog, and there doesn't seem to be much more I can do about it. He is just one of those shaggy individuals – that is how he is.

His mother must have neglected him for she certainly didn't teach him how to wash himself. He keeps his white face and white vest fairly bright but the rest is usually barkit with dubs and muck.

The moment he is finished his work he flops down in the nearest puddle and then the mud dries into tangles which I am constantly cutting off.

Occasionally, I have tried to tackle his coat with a curry comb, but he has got wise and runs as soon as he sees it in my hand. In addition to this problem, he seems permanently to be casting his hair.

I didn't buy him I just acquired him – so I have nobody to blame but myself. He was a young dog when his previous owner cleared off and left him in our dog shed. His name is either Shep or Gyp – nobody is very sure. Neither is he.

In his first few months with us he used to wander off, get picked up by the police and placed in a kennel. Each time we reported him missing he had already been found. When we went to collect him he gave no sign of recognition, such as a wag of his tail, and the police would ask if I was sure he was my dog. That used to annoy me slightly. As if I would want to fake ownership of a mutt like Shep! At the time, I had two perfectly good dogs and could well have done without this very disinterested tyke. Still, I knew nobody else would claim him and he really didn't deserve to be put down.

Maybe if I had sought to train him to my ways at the beginning, he would not have acquired so many bad habits. However, the two other dogs were very well accustomed to our work and, naturally, we used them. In that respect, I was no better or worse than many shepherds nowadays.

Either they don't have the time or maybe they no longer need the money but, certainly, fewer and fewer bother to train on young dogs for sale. In many cases, they rely on their employer to provide them with a dog already fully trained.

It takes many hours of patient handling to get a dog to obey even the basic commands of "sit", "come to heel", "go bye". Then there is the hurdle of introducing it to sheep or cattle. Not all the sheep dogs will work cattle. Shep will, but he is just as orra with them as with sheep.

He makes a tolerable outrun if sent off by the left and will nearly surround the flock. But, at the last minute, he will cut in front of a few and cause them to run in the wrong direction. I think he does this deliberately so that he can waste time chasing each one individually.

He always reminds me of a well-known North-east character who had a dog to sell. It was a hopeless worker, but he was determined to show it off to a potential buyer. The dog went round the sheep reasonably well. The seller anticipated that it would then cut through the middle of the flock, so he shouted: "Divide". The dog duly obliged and the farmer turned to his buyer, exclaiming: "There noo! There's nae mony dogs can dae that!"

Shep's concentration threshold is very low. He quickly gets fed up working and prefers to sit watching his shadow in a wheel hubcap, or try biting the tyre of a passing tractor.

Chasing the farm cats is his favourite pastime although he has never bitten one. Even the kittens are not very frightened of him and sometimes stand their ground, hissing and spitting back.

I've never had a self-feed dog before, but Shep helps himself to whatever milk he needs from the calves' pail. Then he satisfies his appetite at the ever-open bag of dog mixtures. He is not greedy though, and the bag lasts a long time.

During the winter, when we have about five hundred feeding lambs on the farm, there is a lot of work for Shep. If we can keep him on the job for five hours at a stretch, he stops his orra working and uses his energies quite effectively. Sometimes on a gather he can even show style in his forward creep.

I am full of admiration for sheepdog handlers who can eliminate all a dog's bad habits and bring it on to compete in sheepdog trials. Pat Cowie of Tollo Farm, Turriff – a man who has done so much for trialling both as competitor and judge – tells me that only about one in every hundred sheepdogs has the potential to become a trial dog.

Top-class animals, therefore, have a great scarcity value and change hands at prices between £1,000 and £2,000. The asking price for an ordinary working collie capable of handling a large flock is around £600. Some time ago a shepherd from the Borders was selling a dog that had performed well at the trials. He was offered £1,000 by a visiting Irish farmer but refused to sell. Later in the day, he sold the dog to an English farmer for £700.

The Irishman was furious when he heard of the deal, stormed up to the shepherd and shouted: "I'll have you up in front of the Race Relations Board. What do you mean by turning down my better offer?".

"Now, calm down," said the shepherd quietly. "Yon dog's a homer. He has some chance of getting home across the Border – but none of swimming across the Irish Sea!"

What value could I put on Shep? Well, it wouldn't be high. If he got a wage packet at the end of the week, there would be a dismissal notice along with it. I'll just have to put up with the orra brute but I wish he wouldn't nuzzle my neck with his wet nose when I'm driving the Land Rover.

Ach well, I think he is trying to say he likes me, the puir, dishevelled craitur.

I often had to dance to Big Annie's tune

"Fancy you forgetting," said Sandy, shaking his head.

I had just planted myself on one of the comfortable chairs round the auction ring at Thainstone Market and there on the next chair sat my long-time friend and fellow farmer, Sandy McIntosh, from Craig Farm in the shadow of the Knock hill.

I was going to call him my old friend but, of course, people the same age as oneself are never old. "What have I forgotten, Sandy?", I puzzled, thinking I had neglected to bring him a calf or something.

"Hiv ye really forgotten that it was me who helped ye stuff that bicycle tyre wi' grass? And hiv ye forgotten the tyave we had getting it back on its rim?"

Regular readers of this column will recall that two weeks ago I told of returning to Grange dancehall at 3am after seeing a lassie home and finding my hind wheel flat. I had seven miles to cycle home. I know some readers thought I was telling a tall tale – some have told me so – but there beside me was the one person in the world who could verify my story. And to be truthful, I *had* forgotten his valuable assistance.

Sandy had been cycling from Keith to Grange while I was walking in the opposite direction. In the half dark of a summer dawn, he spotted me with my bike upside down in a field gateway, struggling to get the tyre off. With his help, I eventually got mobile. I have since heard of folk similarly stuffing motor bike tyres and even car tyres in emergencies. Because the Grange dance was virtually at Sandy's back door, doubtless he had gone to Keith to survey some different "talent". Maybe he was "going steady", as we said in those days.

We young farm loons worked hard most evenings, but on Friday and Saturday nights, we squeeried the countryside on our bikes, calling in at various dances. Very few people had cars and, in any case, petrol was strictly rationed. Our precious petrol coupons were for essential journeys only.

Even dry batteries for bicycle lamps were scarce. Many of us used gas lamps. These gave off a better light and had the added advantage that you could heat your hands on them. However, they were fikey to handle and it was easy to drown your gas by letting too much water drip on it.

An acquaintance told me of the time he drooned his gas before reaching the dance and craftily raided some other lamps for a knot or two of dry carbide. When the time came to see a lassie home, he discovered, much to his consternation, that one of the lamp's he'd pinched from was her's.

Unlike today's poor deprived youngsters who can only shuffle about to appalling music, my generation took their dancing seriously. Some liked Old Time, others preferred ballroom dancing. Regardless of the venue or of which band was playing, a good combination of both kinds of dancing was guaranteed.

Real efforts were made to mix the company as much as possible. For this purpose, dances such as the Paul Jones were ideal. At the end of one dance, the ladies would form an inner circle which moved clockwise while the men formed an outer circle going anti-clockwise. When the music stopped, the person nearest you was your partner for the next section of the dance.

The dance programme offered infinite variety. Often it started with a Grand March and Circassian Circle. That gave everybody a chance to see who else was there that evening. Next would come an Old Fashioned Waltz followed by, say, a quickstep. The quickstep was my own particular favourite, and many happy times I enjoyed taking the floor to such rousing numbers as *When the Saints Go Marching In.*

Next on the list would be a slow foxtrot, a nice smoochy dance with melodic tunes – often the latest hits – our equivalent of *Top of the Pops.* A more energetic Scottish dance usually followed – perhaps an eightsome reel or, if the company was older, a Lancers. The Lancers was quite complicated, with four distinctly separate setts danced to different tempos. To let everybody get their breath back, something like a foxtrot came next. Ten to one it would be a ladies' choice.

I used to dread being asked up by one big lass called Annie. A farmer's daughter, she was sure to be a great catch for some young farmer but please, I used to think, not this one. To say she was sonsy was putting it mildly:

Remember, laddie, you'll have her for keeps
And a' that she'll speak aboot will be tatties an' neeps.

It was a warning I took to heart in her case. I was accustomed to doing the leading in dances, but not with Annie. Up and down the hall she and I would wrestle for the lead. It was like two Olympic Judo experts battling for supremacy. I usually had to settle for the silver medal.

But I started to get fly. I would ask her which village dance she was going to the next week – then I'd make sure to head off in the opposite direction.

After the interval, the programme was rather similar to the first half but, instead of the eightsome, there would be a Strip the Willow, a Gay Gordons, or maybe a Highland Schottishe. Other more exotic challenges like the tango, the conga and the Palais Glide provided welcome variety.

With the second half of the evening under way, there came the serious business of deciding which lass you would ask to see home. The first one might refuse, and you'd have to go down your list of preferences.

Drawing a total blank was a terrible blow to one's ego, but it did get you home to your bed earlier. The girls of my day had very definite views as to whom they preferred. Dancing and courting were important parts of life which often took all night – as Sandy and I discovered long ago.

I think, Sandy, that I'm 45 years late, but I'd like to say thanks for your help with the bike. And sincere thanks, too, for proving that this scribbler doesn't tell tall tales.

When broken crockery was hit for hens

I've broken my brose bowl. One minute it was nicely wrapped up in a towel on top of the gas fire and the next it was in three bits on the carpet.

I like to let my brose sweat or cook for ten minutes after I have stirred it, so I put a plate on top of the bowl and then cover the lot with a tea towel. Somehow or other it overbalanced and hit the stone kerb. The thing had been showing cracks for ages and it owes me nothing as I've had it for years.

Fortunately, the average ironmonger still sells bowls such as the one I had, so what am I going on about? Well, I'm sad that I can no longer make use of the pieces. In the days when we kept hens, broken crockery like my bowl was carefully hammered into lames, then broken down into even smaller bits. These were put in the grit box for the hens to eat and not one piece was wasted. Strangely enough, hens would eat the broken lames in preference to either limestone grit or shell grit.

Hammers are always fascinating to little boys and the chapping of crockery was about the only time you could use one without getting a row from your parents. I found that out the hard way.

My father had a watch that stayed in a drawer. It had doors at both back and front and I think it was silver. Certainly the back was inscribed silver, but the front was gold with gold numbers on a face which opened. To my knowledge it never worked, but maybe it wasn't wound up regularly.

When I was about three years old I decided one day that I would get it to go. I didn't have to ponder over my chosen method or tool. There were one or two impressive examples of how to go about mending things. For instance, the farm men succeeded in making their ploughs and harrows work by using a hammer on them. And in the bicycle shop, the man always took the trusty hammer to make my sister's bike go better. Surely the watch could be sorted the same way?

I had hit it gently only once or twice when one of my sisters clyped on me. It was the 1930s and nobody had told parents that they shouldn't smack their children. As usual, my mother would wait for no explanation and she skelped me thoroughly. What was worse, she told my father when he came home from his milk round and he skelped me as well. He must have been fond of that watch because that was the one and only skelping he ever gave me.

If my sister hadn't clyped in the first place, I would have put the watch back in the drawer in good working order. I suppose she was just jealous of my prowess with the hammer. The girls liked broken dishes for their "hoosies", whereas I was authorised to hammer them into hens' grit. The hens needed them to help grind down the corn in their gizzards. In later years, when I had to take my turn at dressing and preparing fowls for the pot, I always opened up the gizzard to see what the bird had been eating. I was often amazed at the size of pebbles it contained.

A wide variety of birds are noticeable at the edges of our roads, picking up little stones to help them grind the seeds and grains which form their staple diet. It is a wonder that the tar on some of the stones don't play merry hell with their metabolism.

Our retail milk round provided a ready outlet for our year-round production of cockerels, hens and ducks. If we had less than thirty to pluck and prepare at the weekend we thought business was slack. Customers would order a certain weight of bird and we liked to have at least three days' notice. Given that, we had time to get the bird just right.

On Thursday night we would choose the fowl from the perches and shut it in a dark box for twenty-four hours to empty its digestive system. Fridays and Saturdays were our principal dressing days and we took a pride in the presentation of the oven-ready bird.

The neck, the liver, the heart and the gizzard were all placed in the cavity of the birds for making soup or chicken stock. There was quite an art in splitting the gizzard with a sharp knife and carefully washing out the grit from that powerful grinding mill of pure muscle. I didn't much care for it myself, but some people used to enthuse about the delicacy of that particular piece of the chicken.

If a customer required a fowl at short notice we would always oblige, but my mother invariably remarked: "Do your customers think that my hens run around with their feathers off?"

We used to think we were doing well if we had cockerels ready for selling at sixteen weeks old. But now, broiler-chicken rearers get their birds to marketing size at sixty days. Small wonder that chicken doesn't taste like it used to. And of course, today's boiling fowls come straight from the battery cages whereas previously all the birds were reared free range with the ability to peck at whatever they chose. Being fed exclusively on meal, poultry have no need of gizzards to grind their grain. Consequently, there is now no place or use for grit or chapped-up crockery.

The fur and feather sections of our agricultural shows are always well attended. It was most encouraging to see so many poultry exhibits this year. The old-fashioned breeds of Light Sussex, Rhode Island Red and many others had strong classes. As only the very best birds in each fancier's flock are exhibited, there must be many people who can still enjoy a good pot of chicken soup, followed by a nice roast fowl for Sunday lunch.

An expert carver, such as my mother was, could make one hen feed fourteen folk and all the kids got a wishbone or something that looked like it. Try that with a broiler.

Clock was his only enemy . . .

Just because I happen to mention my mother quite frequently in my articles I would hate readers to think that she had more influence on my growing years than did my father.

Willie Watt was a compassionate, straightforward man – someone you immediately respected – and a tower of strength to his family. He never said a wrong word about anyone. I remember he and I were hand milking cows side by side one night. I would have been about ten years old at the time and I foolishly related some gossip I'd heard that day. He quietly replied: "If ye canna say onything good aboot somebody, dinna say onything at a'".

He was a difficult man to keep up with because he was always so busy. With hindsight, I can identify his one big fault, he didn't delegate enough and consequently did far too much work himself. He was the original workaholic. One story I heard about him tells it all.

Several of the town's tradesmen were sitting one evening having a quiet dram and a blether. They got around to discussing who might be the busiest person each of them knew. Several candidates were mentioned and their merits assessed. Then Arthur, a long retired tailor, announced: "Well, boys, I think Willie Watt can beat them all. He was the only customer I ever had who would open my shop door and say: 'Aye, aye, Arthur. It's a fine day. Mak' a suit tae me', and shut the door again. No question of material, no question of measurements, just: 'Arthur, mak' a suit tae me'".

From the day he returned wounded from World War I until the day he died, my

father never altered an ounce in weight and so his measurements didn't alter either. His suits were always of hard-wearing tweed, and he got through about three every year.

He delivered milk round Keith twice daily, except on Wednesdays and Sundays when he took time to visit his two outfarms. The farms extended to nearly eight hundred acres, but in the 30s, when I first became aware of them, they carried only a quarter of the animals that they do nowadays.

Power was provided by horses, three pairs on each farm. These big animals and their foals ate a lot of grass. I suppose each adult horse ate as much as three cows. It was important that the fields which the horses grazed were not manured. Fertilised grass was blamed for causing the dreaded grass sickness that killed so many horses in their prime.

An unbroken three-year-old colt could be bought for £60 and a well-trained four-year-old gelding, ready to start carting work in a city, fetched £120. There was useful profit to be made then, if the horses could only be kept healthy. Sadly, most years we had our casualties and I can still recall with horror the sickly smell that prevaded the loosebox of a horse in its death throes with grass sickness. It needed four men digging for half a day to bury a dead horse, and that was a hindrance to the rush of spring work.

My father managed to shrug off losses remarkably well, or so it seemed at the time. After tractors had replaced the horses on our farms in the 50s, he would often say that the fields were lonely places of an evening without the horses to say hello to.

He used to tell us lads that anybody can do anything if they set their mind to it. He was the world's eternal optimist, although he had doubts at times about Churchill's strategies in World War II. The lack of vision among our generals in World War I appalled him, and he openly blamed Churchill for the failure of the Dardanelles campagin.

We often entertained guests in our big farmhouse. Some were paying guests, others just friends visiting. A crowded table for Sunday dinner was the norm. We could take sixteen comfortably, but often there were more.

On one memorable occasion, one of our guests was asked why he had never married. He replied that this wasn't the right time to tie the knot. My father was a small man and normally very quiet. But he drew himself up to his full height in his seat at the end of the table and boomed: "It is never the right time. It is never the right time to change jobs. It is never the right time to start a business. It is never the right time to take a holiday. It is never the right time to get married. It is never the right time to start a family. Balderdash. Stuff and nonsense". My parents got an invitation to that gentleman's wedding within a year.

Although he had no great love of the internal combustion engine, he thought the introduction of electricity was absolutely marvellous. To begin with, we had our own generating set driven by the same water wheel that drove the threshing mill. It charged row upon row of big batteries. These battery cells were very similar to the wet batteries required to power folk's wireless sets, only ten times as big. By the by, why did we need a dry battery as well as a wet battery for the wireless?

Later on, we coupled up the Lister engine that operated our first milking machines, but even then we generated only sufficient power to provide lights. The arrival of grid power from the North of Scotland Hydro Electric Board (or the Grampian Electricity Co as it was in those early days) was a great day in all our lives. My father often praised the wonderful service provided by the linesmen who somehow kept the current flowing even in the severest storms.

I suppose my father's consideration for others was his greatest hallmark. He helped many a family through the hungry 30s. Times started to get better in 1939 as the country began to spend money on re-armaments. Men found jobs again, and debts that my father had long forgotten were repaid in full by grateful customers. Where previously he had been content if he ended a financial year £200 better off than he started, in 1939 he had £1,500 more than he could account for in sold produce.

He had infinite patience with children. At least two generations of girls and boys had a "hurl" along their street on his milk cart. And there was often an extra paillie of milk for a particularly peely-wally bairn. His nickname, "Cauley's", was derived from the farm of Cauldhame (Coldhome) where he had once been a tenant. Although he changed farms, the name stuck.

With a cheery word for everyone, he used to hurry through his twice-daily milk rounds, a happy man at peace with himself and the world. His only enemy was the clock. Throughout my life, I have tried to adhere to the constant advice he gave my brother and me: "Never stick". A simple philosophy, but a wise one.

Service with a smile . . .

"Are we expecting royalty?" That was the quip I got from one of my men when I asked him to swipe some dubs. Sorry, I mean sweep some mud. With so many livestock in the farmyard of a winter a fair accumulation of mud is inevitable. Our steading stands on ground with very little slope in it, and consequently the water lies around most of the winter unless swept away.

"Yes," I replied, "only my royalty happens to be a customer". While those of us on the farm are well accustomed to mud, I don't think it is reasonable to expect someone to step out of a clean car and find themselves ankle deep in dubs. Not everyone lives in wellies like dairy folk do.

By commandeering the tractor mounted scraper, which is used each day to sweep the muck from the cubicle house, it is fairly easy to keep the farm close moderately clean. We seldom have to revert to the use of brush and shovel as we had to in the days of the horse and cart.

To my way of thinking, customers and potential customers are extremely important people and should be pandered to. I could rear the most wonderful cattle in the world, but if I didn't have customers for them I would quickly be out of business.

Not everyone has the temperament to serve the public, but it has always been second nature to me. I suppose my boyhood background of milk retailing instilled in me the need to establish good relations with your customers. I still genuinely enjoy dealing with people. If I come across a surly shopkeeper or shop assistant I just don't go back to that shop.

Like every milk roundsman, I had a fair number of milkboys and trotters through my hands. If a boy could make the grade as a good trotter, he would be certain to succeed in later life – especially if his chosen employment involved serving the public. I have been impressed by the many who have achieved success in teaching, as policemen, commercial travellers shopkeepers and tradesmen. Because they learned the business early, they are totally at ease when dealing with the public – and it shows.

Maybe it should be a pre-requisite for those entering the Civil Service that they have previously served the public in one capacity or another. I am not for one moment suggesting that all civil servants are rude, but too many are less helpful than they might be.

It is my proud boast that in my seven years as a milkman I only once had to be rude to a housewife and ask her to take her custom elsewhere. It gave me no pleasure. Again, in my five years as a Member of Parliament I only once was rude to a constituent – but it gave me a great deal of pleasure that time.

The extremely wealthy old gent wrote to me complaining about a tradesman's bill that he considered too steep. He asked me what I proposed to do about it. To me, the bill seemed perfectly reasonable, and I told him so in the same snooty vein as he had written to me. Well, he was so mad that he sent the correspondence to a Sunday paper which duly printed it. I wouldn't have minded that one whit if the news editor had troubled to ask me for my side of the story, but he didn't.

Unlike newspaper-delivery boys, who work their rounds alone, the milkboys work together and sometimes start to play around. Tradesmen used to have a saying that one boy is a boy, two boys are half a boy, and three boys are no boy at all. That could often be the case unless the roundsman exerted discipline.

I think present-day society is poorer for the demise of the delivery men. When a wide variety of mobile services were on the streets, neighbours would meet together at the baker's van, the butcher's van or the grocer's van. A friendly gossip for a few minutes made a welcome break from the lonely routine of housework. Advice of all kinds was passed from one to the other, and if any elderly neighbour did not appear at the van two neighbours would make it their business to find out if anything was wrong. Nowadays, the doctor's surgery provides the only meeting place some people have.

I remember one butcher who had both a town and a country round. He knew everything that was going on in the community, yet he could never have been called nosey. He had a great knack of knowing which young lad was looking for an apprenticeship, and he could fix a housewife up with a school-leaving lassie who was looking for a housemaid's job. He fixed up more young people with jobs than ever the careers officer did, and there was no paperwork involved.

Wages for school leavers were maybe low, but there seemed to be more job satisfaction around than there is today. One young girl had a job working with horses. At a dance one night, her pals were chiding her for working for such low wages. I shall always remember her reply: "Look! I like my job so much that if I had the money I would pay the boss to be allowed to work for her. Can any of the rest of you say that?".

Another young girl I knew of had been working as a housemaid for a couple of years when one day her mistress said: "Mary, I'm sorry to tell you that my husband has got a new job and we will be moving to Galashiels. Will you come with us?" "Aye, fairly. Faur is't?" Mary responded, without lifting her head from scrubbing the kitchen table.

I'm heart sorry to see young lads with no work to go to. They hang around the streets all day and it is small wonder they get up to some devilment in the evening. Every young creature has surplus energy to work off if they are to go tired to their beds at night. The fault lies with our society, not with the youngsters. It is downright crazy that politicians cannot devise a method of harnessing the energies of our youth for the benefit of the young people themselves and of the public at large.

Farm mill days were long and hard . . .

Well, that's the harvest finished for another year.

It is always a great relief to see the grain safely in the bins in the grain store. The barley bins are full to the top and the wheat bins are heaped high above the extra shelvings added to give greater capacity.

Despite the wet weather that dominated late August and most of September, we have managed to combine most of the fields at the right stage. Overall, the moisture content has been sixteen per cent or less and only one bin of barley has had to be dried. A strong fan dries the grain by blowing hot air up through the perforated iron floors of the bins.

Only the oat crop has produced a disappointing yield. It was grown in the poorest field on the farm and in addition, it got badly puddled by heavy rain shortly after the seed was sown. As is usual in such cases, the weeds grew apace. Without a strong application of weedkiller, we wouldn't have had any crop at all.

Although the yield is less than hoped for, we have a bonny sample of oats which we're tempted to try on the market. Apparently Finland has had a disastrously wet summer and many of their crops have failed completely. Merchants are offering £120 a ton for oats to ship to Finland in the next few weeks, before the Baltic freezes over.

If the amount of berries on the rowan trees are anything to go by, we could be in for a severe winter. Some of the rowan trees have already lost their leaves and are a mass of bright red berries from top branch to bottom. The fieldfares will dine well if we do not have an early frost. It strikes me as strange that not a newspaper has talked of global warming this summer. The phenomenon cannot have gone away this quickly – if it ever was there, that is.

When I look at the grain in the bins awaiting transportation in the merchants' lorries or, in our case, mostly ready to be crushed for cattle feed, I cannot but marvel at the tremendous advantages that the combine harvester and the grain drier have brought to our way of life.

Much has been written in nostalgic fashion about the harvests of long ago, but people generally forget that when the harvest itself was over, only half the work had actually been done. Once the ricks were safely built, thatched and roped, the constant grind of carting sheaves, threshing and carting both grain and straw was just beginning.

Most farms had a barn mill powered by water from the mill dam. Those places without a generous water supply had to rely on a horse-driven mill and later, an engine-driven mill. While the barn mills could cope with the daily feed requirement of the cattle and the many farm horses, a visit from the travelling steam mill was necessary several times a year to thresh barley or oats for selling.

There was an air of excitment about the place when the big black monster with its huge iron wheels came puffing up the brae. On the steep ascent to our farm, a big head of steam was needed to enable the traction engine to pull its train of threshing mill and high trailer. However, they always seemed to have power aplenty and the mill man had huge wooden chocks to put behind the wheels if the driver called for a halt. The hours worked by the engine driver and his mill man were quite outrageous when seen in the context of the eight-hour day, plus overtime. There was no talk of overtime for anyone in those days. The men just worked on until the job was done.

The mill man was always first on the go in the morning. He raked out the cold ashes, then lit the fire in the firebox before going to the farm kitchen for breakfast.

By eight o'clock the threshing squad had arrived. This would consist of the farm staff, perhaps some casual workers, and usually the neighbouring farmers – who would expect a like number of men to turn up at their forthcoming mill day.

As well as seeing to the needs of the hungry beast by fuelling it constantly with coal and water throughout the day, the driver and his mate took it in turns to feed the mill with sheaves. These were passed to them by the two eident "lowsers", who cut the sheaf bands and made sure that each sheaf was pointing the right way for feeding into the mill mouth. By the time every sheaf from eight ricks had been triple-handed, all those strong men and women involved were really tired.

Very often, however, the mill men had yet another big job to do. It was their task to deliver the day's thresh on their big wagon to the local mill or, in the case of barley, to the nearest distillery. Mostly, these jobs were done in the dark and it is really little wonder that mill men sought to enhance their calorie intake by having a dram or two – or three – on the road.

Stories of the mill men and their drinking are legion throughout the North-east. The one I like best concerns Davie, who drove a threshing mill for Mr Reid of Banff. After delivering two loads of barley to a local distillery and downing a strong dram each time, Davie called into a nearby pub for a beer.

By the time he emerged, he was very definitely fu'. He tried to drive his steam engine with its empty wagon, but steered it into a ditch. The big wheels started spinning and Davie just couldn't get grip for them. Tiredness eventually overcame him and he fell fast asleep at the side of the ditch.

A passing motorist saw the predicament and informed the mill owner. When Mr Reid arrived on the scene just before midnight, there was the steam engine with the wheel still spinning and Davie snoring brawly. He shook his man awake and said loudly: "Now Davie, ye ken I canna dae wi' this drinking". "Well, Mr Reid", said Davie, "if ye canna da wi' drinking ye'll jist hae tae tak less o't". With that, he promptly went back to sleep.

They were hardy boys, though, these threshing-mill operators. Without fail,

Davie, his mill man, the steam engine, the threshing mill and the wagon all drew in to a farm close three miles away at six in the morning, ready to start another long, hard day's work.

Sold on a centre of excellence

Nothing succeeds like success.

To find the proof of that, we need look no further than the well-established Thainstone Agricultural Centre.

When the directors of Aberdeen and Northern Marts took the bold decision to centre operations at Thainstone, near Inverurie, even the most optimistic of their number could not have foreseen just how busy it would become.

Latterly, all farmers knew that the days of the Kittybrewster marts were numbered. Selling cattle at these sites near Aberdeen city centre generated an extra build-up of traffic on a Friday which led to serious congestion on the streets.

The farmers themselves faced additional inconvenience through having to dodge the busy traffic as they moved from the Central Mart to the Belmont Mart or Kittybrewster Mart.

Virtually everyone was relieved to be relocated on the secluded site at Inverurie, where parking for cars and lorries posed no problem. I just wish the roads department at the Scottish Office had shown equal foresight and dualled all of the Inverurie bypass. That would have made the new set-up near perfect.

The company itself made a mistake in the early days by failing to consult its members adequately on the timing of closures of the old local markets. But that is all in the past. The high numbers of cattle and sheep coming forward for sale thoughout the past year, and especially this autumn, justifies the heavy outlay.

For the first time, the farming industry in the North-east has a market showpiece that we can all be proud of. Thainstone is certainly a place where the non-farming public can call to have their education improved.

With the sale rings laid out like an amphitheatre and the overhead viewing gangways in the pen area, there is no chance of getting knocked over by a passing cow, or savaged by a sheep. Personally, I have enjoyed going to Thainstone. And now I go there with a growing sense of pride in being a part of its success – however small a part.

Usually when I attend a sale I am involved either in buying or selling. However, the other Saturday I took a busman's holiday and went to see the sale of rare breeds. The place was mobbed, but the facilities proved more than adequate. All the ample car parks were full to capacity, but an adjoining field was pressed into service. Thainstone must be about the only place where free parking is still the rule.

The normal Saturday sheep sale was also in full swing. Two sale rings were coping with 11,500 lambs and ewes. Viewed from the raised gangways, it was a veritable sea of sheep. I couldn't help but marvel at the sheer logistics of clocking all of them into the pens.

Getting each pen of sheep to the correct ring at the correct place on the catalogue doesn't happen by chance. Incidentally, sheep numbers have increased still further at the Saturday sales and extra pens have had to be "hired". I must pay tribute to the management, but more particularly to the many yardsmen for the magnificent job they do week after week. Almost all of the yardsmen have a

farming background and they get the animals moving in the right direction with none of the bawling and shouting that is common in other markets.

Only a small section of the vast penning area was used for the rare breeds sale. Nevertheless, that was the area attracting most attention. The collection of cattle, sheep, goats, pigs, poultry, pigeons and rabbits was a joy to behold.

There were lots of children there, all getting an education in comparing one breed with another. Many of them were very knowledgeable about their own particular animals and well accustomed to handling livestock.

It's easy for we conventional farmers to scoff at the hobby farmers in our midst, but they certainly give their kids a wonderful opportunity to handle a wide variety of livestock. They have horses, cattle, sheep, pigs and poultry around the farm – just as it was in the days when I wore short breeks. I know I enjoyed such a childhood, but I can only show my grandchildren cows and sheep in large numbers.

I have to confess that I spent quite a bit of my day off watching a sale of antique farm implements and accessories. Held in the spacious concourse or atrium, the sale had a very different atmosphere from the usual farm roup that take place in a draughty corner of the farm steading. I saw an old bicycle gas lamp sell for £48, while two lowsin's knives for use at a threshing mill fetched £10 each. Being no hoarder myself, I have no wish to own such artefacts.

Things agricultural are not the only goings-on at Thainstone. The roomy sale hall that had seen the rare breeds in the afternoon was by ten at night the venue for a rave which lasted until six the following morning.

Now, I know nothing about raves. Ought I to be ashamed of myself? I think maybe in this case ignorance is bliss. These kids bounced up and down for eight hours on a concrete floor while their eardrums were hammered almost to destruction. If, as a farmer, I tried to keep animals in such conditions I would be prosecuted. Certainly, a high percentage of them would develop pneumonia.

Sunday forenoon sees the same floorspace used for a market. Some eighty traders do business from 10am until 5pm. Then, if you wander into that arena on a Monday evening, you'll find a car auction in progress. It is to be hoped that all these varied functions help to contribute to the high cost of running such a large establishment.

Farmers are constantly being told to diversify. Well, our mart company has done it. Anyday now they will be able to sell you an oilrig by electronic auction.

I haven't mentioned the many shops and banks around the concourse, but please call and see for yourself. The pleasant coffee stall and the large open restaurant upstairs will provide you with a snack or a meal. Mind you, I doubt if the restaurant serves vegetarian dishes, but the meats and the fish are highly recommended.

And you can get skirlie with everything. Fond as I am of oatmeal, I can't eat skirlie, but my son assures me it is delicious.

So next time you are on the A96, cry in by Thainstone. You might go home the proud owner of a really ugly, cuddly Vietnamese pot-bellied pig for as little as £9.

Ploughing on with the crop work

It is ploughing time again.

No sooner is harvest finished than we're into sowing the winter crops of rape, barley and wheat. I just happen to have an intense dislike of winter rape, so I don't grow any. The fields of bright, almost luminous yellow are somehow offensive to my eye.

This particular crop wouldn't be grown at all if it weren't for the huge EC subsidy, and that fact annoys me. If I had anything to do with negotiating between the EC and the US on the vexed question of GATT (the General Agreement on Tariff and Trade), I would concede to the US the right to supply Europe with soya bean meal. After all, the States can grow soya much more cheaply than Europe can grow winter rape. The edible oils and the protein cattle feeds produced by rape and by soya are very similar.

In return, I would demand that the Yanks stop rabbiting on about their right to supply Europe with grain. With our higher yields an acre of wheat and barley, we have no need to import subsidised US grain. And anyway, both countries should be giving away five per cent of production to the starving people of the world.

We have come a long way in grain production from our grandfathers' times. As I've mentioned before, their projected yields were: "Ane tae saw, ane tae maw (eat), and ane te pey the laird witha". They therefore expected only a threefold increase over their sowing rate. There is little doubt that part of the reason for our success in growing grain stems from our expertise in ploughing.

Much of the prairie land in the US gets only surface cultivation, or at best light ploughing. By contrast, our fields benefit from a good furr(ow) – usually about ten inches in depth. All the trash or filth from last year's crop is turned well down into the bottom of the deep furrow where it gradually rots to provide mulch and nutrients for next year's crop.

We have seen many revolutions in farming methods over the centuries, but a Roman of 66 BC would recognise a mould board plough. Where his single furrow plough was drawn by a team of four oxen, our five-furrow implements get pulled by one hundred horse-power tractors.

Our national poet, Robbie Burns, tells of ploughing five roods of land in a long, hard working day. That was five-eights of an acre. We must presume that his "guid mare Meg" was harnessed with a heavier horse.

I am not sufficiently acquaint with the history of the Clydesdale horse to know if Clydesdales were around in Robbie's day. But I do know that the Ayrshire cow breed had been developed by that time.

Some years ago, when on a delegation to Finland, I learned that Ayrshire cows had been exported to both Finland and Norway during Robbie's lifetime. The breed proved so successful that today, eighty per cent of all Finnish dairy cows are pure Ayrshires.

Many ploughman derive great satisfaction from ploughing. "It is good for the soul", one told me. As for myself, I am content to see a good, deep furrow and the ground getting blackened quickly, as they say.

Even after the recent prolonged and heavy rain, the soil is turning up remarkably dry. In fact, when first turned up our ploughed land is the colour of dark chocolate, rather than black.

If the weather stays dry the furrows will quickly dry out or "hair up", and change to the colour of milk chocolate. The land is then given the minimum of cultivation to produce a friable surface. A contractor subsequently drills the barley and wheat seeds about an inch deep, and we harrow it over.

Now, I know that plenty farmers had their crops sown weeks ago but here at sea level we prefer to wait a bit. If the crop ripens too early, the crows and pigeons come from miles around. Many farmers have given up growing winter barley because of bird damage.

In summer, my son and I take it in turns to get up early to scare the birds away from the ripening barley. We find that if we persist for about two hours after daylight, the birds get fed up and go elsewhere in search of food for most of that day. Usually there is a further period of about an hour before darkness falls when the crop needs to be protected from the returning birds.

Well, if it's ploughing time again it is also ploughing match time. Throughout Scotland, enthusiasts gather at ploughing matches to compete against each other.

In general, they are more concerned with the look of their furrows than with the amount of ground turned over. Many of these dedicated professionals go on to excel at national and international level.

I have never been able to get excited about ploughing matches but each to his own taste. These events can still draw crowds eager to see the horse ploughs, the old tractor ploughs and the modern outfits compete in their respective classes. Each ploughman has a helper to keep him right, to ensure that not a trace of green grass shows through the well set-up furrows.

The story goes that in the old days, one ploughman and his assistant competed regularly at their local horse ploughing match for nigh on fifty years. The first Thursday in December was the sacrosanct date. Well, this particular year Sandy and Geordie was getting on fine, though Geordie was a bit quiet. About two o'clock a funeral cortege passsed the field where the ploughing match was being held. Geordie pulled up the horses, took his hands off the stilts of the plough, removed his cap and stood with his head bowed while the hearse went by.

Sandy couldn't contain his anger and surprise. He shouted to Geordie, asking what the hell he meant by ruining their chances of a prize. "Aye, maybe so, Sandy", replied Geordie quietly, "but she wis a guid wife tae me these mony years".

Threat from monster in woods

It was a sunny afternoon in July when I visited the Forestry Commission open day at the Bin Hill forest near Huntly.

The display was most impressive and merited immediate comment. Yet I held off putting pen to paper. I had hoped that the passage of time would reduce the sense of shock I experienced that Saturday afternoon.

Botany has never been my strong subject, so I am not qualified to discourse on the various kinds of conifer trees being grown at the Bin. For sheer beauty, I cannot see past the larches with their fine tracery of branchlets and their colouring. In early spring, the delicate green of the tiny new needles always delights me.

These change to a bonny reddish brown in the autumn just before they are shed. And even on a dreich winter's day, the purple sheen of larch branches adds colour to the otherwise dull, dark green forest scene created by most of the other varieties.

The businessman in me though, settles for the sitka spruce because they produce marketable timber faster than other species. Many of the sitka trees on view at the open day were growing shoots of more than one metre each year. Provided the long, delicate growth doesn't get threshed and broken by a high wind in July or August, the tree will stretch more than three feet annually and broaden gradually year by year.

I have recently heard of a six-acre stand of spruce on Speyside selling for £120,000. Maybe when farmers are young they should plant trees so that they can have a pension fund to cash when they retire.

Several varieties of trees are ready for thinning at twenty-five to thirty years and in line for clear fell at forty-five to fifty-five years. The latest fetish for growing hardwoods may be all very asthetic, but these trees will never be cost effective.

I must be mellowing with age, because until recently I was adamant that forestry and livestock farming don't mix. My own attempts at tree-growing ranged from middling success to downright failure. Although a conifer wood makes good shelter for outwintering cattle, the trees do not like their shallow roots disturbed. In addition, they can't stand animals rubbing against them and many will die if cattle roam among them for several winters.

Planting seemed to be the obvious solution for some of our wet land, but in the rush of summer work we never got round to weeding the young trees. They took several years to beat the grass which grew undisturbed around them. Then one very stormy winter, some hungry Blackface ewes used a snow drift to climb over the protecting fence. In one night, the brutes devoured all the growing shoots of the two foot trees. The survivors from the original 6,000 took years to recover and all have twists or bends.

That experience convinced me that only a dedicated forester should attempt to grow trees. Yet, in recent years we can see several woodlands in the North-east that have been successfully established by farmers. A bankrupt nation like Britain desperately needs as much home-grown timber as can be produced. I don't care who owns the trees as long as they get grown.

Woodlands wonderer . . . Hamish, from being adamant that forestry and livestock farming don't mix, ponders the future after the establishment of woodlands on North-east farms. "Britain desperately needs as much home-grown timber as can be produced", he says.

A lot of first class timber was on display at the Bin Hill forest (which is more than one hundred years old). Some of the trees are the third crop grown on the ground and wildlife abounds among the many varieties. While the foresters were well pleased with the turnout of spectators, I felt that many more members of the public would have benefited from a visit.

Without doubt, it was the first sighting of the monster of the woods that made the greatest impression on me. I know many people have seen the tree-felling machine on television, but being close up to it in the forest was quite awe-inspiring.

Here was a German/Finnish machine that grasped the tree, felled it, stripped off the bark and cut it into lengths in the same time it has taken me to write about it.

Perhaps I can best illustrate my feelings by describing the only other occasion on which I experienced a similar sensation. It was in the early 1970s, when I was privileged to be invited by a Gamrie skipper for a trip on a purse-seine-net boat.

On the second morning, the crew shot their vast net around a shoal of mackerel that had been located by sonar. The area of sea covered was bigger than three football pitches until the net was gradually drawn in. The whole sea teemed with beautiful plump fish.

Eventually, the vacuum pumps were lowered into the net and the fish spewed aboard for hour after hour. More than one hundred and fifty tons of the beauties were taken by our vessel and by two others which had come alongside. None escaped to breed again. As the huge empty net was winched in through big rollers, I couldn't help feeling that the very spirit of the shoal had been crushed. Maybe I was a Red Indian in an earlier existence.

Anyway, the same sense of foreboding came over me in the forest last July and the feeling is still as strong. For me, the mechanical might of the forestry operation brought into question the ethics of present day industry and commerce.

Must we always strive to invent machines which only serve to lengthen dole queues in our towns and cities? Are there to be no jobs for youngsters leaving school? There seems to be little value put on the dignity of labour these days.

I have known many fine men who have spent their lifetime working in the woods. They are a breed with independent spirit and an outlook on life fresher than our own. Maybe I am over-reacting. If we can quadruple the acreage under trees, then maybe there will be work for both men and machines. I certainly hope so, because I felt that that machine wasn't just devouring trees: it was devouring the souls of woodmen, past, present and future.

Ah! Stable smell memories

"Stockman/Tractorman wanted for Nairnshire farm" said a recent advert in the P&J. It's changed days about a farm when you get the tractorman looking after the cattle as well.

In my young day, the horsemen were most indignant if they were asked to come into the byre. They would condescend to lend their weight on a rope in the case of a difficult calving, but otherwise the nearest they came to the smelly place was the neep shed at one end of the building. Only the cattleman and the orra loon tended the cattle. The horses' stable had a different smell altogether.

Although I have been a dedicated cow man all my life I must admit to a special nostalgia for the smell of the stable on a frosty autumn morning. The mixture of odours – fresh horse dung, harness polish, and warm horseflesh mingled with the reek of bogie roll from the newly-kindled pipes of the grieve and the horsemen – remain for me an ever fresh and pleasant memory.

By contrast, the cow byre was mucky and smelly in the morning until it had been mucked out and bedded down with fresh straw.

Today's stockman/tractorman will probably be expected to care for more than one hundred beef cows, or maybe nearer three hundred fattening cattle. The latter will be loose housed in big airy cattle courts, and quite likely the cows will be outwintered in a free-draining field with some tree belts for shelter. The feeding arrangements will include a high degree of mechanisation. Big bales of silage or hay will be carried on the forks of the fore-loader and tipped into a feeding ring. For that reason alone, our stockman also needs to be a tractorman – and a good one at that.

I still haven't got over the shock of seeing that lovely, high-stacking loader at Turriff Show, priced at £28,000 after all discounts. We won't linger on the picture of an amateur driver cowping that lot on a steep, slippery field.

The housed cattle will be fed in long troughs with barriers to prevent them tramping the precious fodder. Their food will arrive in the form of silage blocks cut from a nearby pit. Alternatively, the silage will be mixed with draff and barley and perhaps turnips, in an expensive forage wagon.

Hamish attends a newly-born Simmental calf

These wagons have a high centre of gravity, with augurs and belts delivering a steady stream of feed into the troughs. Again, there is no room for mistakes.

Yet despite all the expensive mechanisation, there will always come a moment when the stockman's special skills will be called upon. Perhaps, a cow having a difficult calving will need expert assistance from the man on the spot. Or maybe a calf that has been born during the night hasn't managed to get its first suck. Only know-how and patient handling will get it on to the teat of a fractious cow or heifer. If the calf is dorby or weak, the stockman may have to milk off a bottleful of colostrum and get it started sucking that way. Calving-time on a stock farm is no place for clock watchers. Many a meal is steen cauld or dried up before it gets eaten.

The present day stockman has a very different task from his predecessor, who generally had no more than thirty tied cattle and thirty loose stirks to tend. But less stock didn't mean less eident work. All the food had to be barrowed along the narrow pass behind the cows.

Barrows and draff hurlies were usually three feet wide. At Birkenburn where I was reared, the door to the draff shed was about eight feet wide. One morning my brother Percy failed to negotiate the turn. Somehow or other, he found the opening too narrow at one side.

The handles of the hurley scraped one side of the door, squashing his fingers between the two hard surfaces. Now, metal and concrete are harder than skin and bone, and he left the points of two fingers sticking to the wall.

Wrapping his hand in a hanky, he finished feeding the cattle and then drove himself to casualty where the doctor trimmed off some more.

Easily the worst job, though was mucking the byres. All the stuff had to be graiped from the greep into barrows, then rowed to a midden which was usually some distance across the farm close. Things weren't so bad when the midden was empty; but soon you were faced with pushing the barrow up a slippery plank, then tipping out its reeking contents.

To cowp it to right or left was easy, but to cowp it over-end was diffficult for a short chiel like me. Some farmers insisted that the dung be spread out on the midden surface each day. Doubtless when the time came for carting it out to the fields, the spread dung was easier to reload than the barrow-deep stuff.

Every midden had a "strang hole" where the bree drained away and ours was no exception. One afternoon a newly born black calf slithered into the deep hole. Fortunately, the mother started bawling and on investigation, I found the poor cratur with nothing but eyes and nose showing above the black sotter.

I've often wished I had learnt to use a lassoo like the cowboys in films do, and never more so than on that afternoon. Plunging into the unholy mess, I secured a halter over the calf's neck. Along came the cattleman and hauled out first the calf, then me.

Judicious washing with cold, then hot water cleaned and revived the calf. However, no amount of washing would remove the smell from my clothes. They were of no further use.

As luck would have it, the Farmers' Ball was taking place that night. Well, I was clean alright, and dressed up in kilt, Prince Charlie jacket, stiff shirt and bow tie. All went well until I started to sweat at an eightsome reel.

Only my mother and sisters would dance with me for the rest of the evening.

Even I could smell myself. I happen to like the smell of cows, but oh, that pong was something powerful. Now, I wonder: does today's stockman/tractorman go home smelling of dung or diesel?

Sharp lesson from the dominie . . .

'Twas the autumm of 1939 and schools hadn't re-opened after summer holidays.

All the school buildings had been commandeered for billeting the territorial soldiers, mobilised just before war was declared in early September.

Our farm had lost two good men to the Army – the first and third horsemen. Finding replacements was almost impossible.

So it was that I found myself, at the age of thirteen-and-a-half, driving the third pair. Before then, I had done my share of gathering and binding sheaves behind a scyther, and I'd also taken my turn at redding roads round the outside of the fields. But driving three horses in the binder was a prestigious job that had previously been jealously guarded by the first three horsemen.

I quickly mastered the technique and the horses worked well for me. There were fewer breakdowns with my McCormick binder than with the much newer International being drive by the second horseman (now foreman).

I was well accustomed to handling horses, and my only real drawback was in having to stand on a box to get the heavy collars over their heads. Still, provided I started a few minutes earlier than the other lads, I had my pair harnessed and ready to leave the stable at yokin time.

The oat crops that year were very uneven in length, and it was essential to make constant adjustments to the five levers on the binder in order to attain even-bottomed sheaves with the twine in the proper place. I took great pains to get my sheaves just right; and after the second day I was promoted over the new second horseman – an older man who hated the binder.

September and October were wet and it was a slow, difficult harvest. Although the soldiers had long since marched to war and the schools were functioning again, I was fully occupied leading sheaves to the cornyard. By the time we had finished harvest it was early November. I was doing a man's work and looking forward to getting a start with the plough.

At that time boys were allowed to apply for an exemption to leave school three months before their fourteen birthday. Despite my mother's protestations, and the advice of my three elder sisters, who were taking further education, I decided to leave school. My father was ambivalent. After all, he still hadn't found a replacement third horseman.

One Monday I duly presented myself at the headmaster's door with my books in my arms. Mr Drimmie was busy and said he'd see me later. Eventually he called me from the Latin class and I made my request for an exemption to work on the farm.

He was a powerfully-build man, was Mr Drimmie, with the hairiest hands and arms I had ever seen. And in answer to my request, I felt the full force of his physical strength. He gave me such a belt on the chin that I fell in a heap in the corridor. As I struggled to my feet he boomed: "You will leave my school with your Highers and not before". That was my introduction to "careers guidance". Nobody argued with headmasters in those days, so I gritted my teeth and settled back into school routine.

Hamish addressing students at Aberdeen University – he was Rector there for four years from 1984

In the following three years I acquired a love of learning which I have never lost. With the shortage of labour on the farm and the cows to be milked three times a day, there was little time for homework. I had to acquire the habit of reading and putting my thoughts and ideas down on paper very quickly.

I left school with modest Highers, a liking for study and, most importantly, an RAF scholarship to St Andrews University and accelerated entry into the Air Force. Still, I would have appreciated more careers guidance than I received.

I believe that guidance should begin in the first year of secondary schooling, before choice of subjects is made. It is important that pupils identify which career sector they wish to enter – for example, the caring professions or administration, the production sector or the financial sector.

In my own case, I would have preferred not to have been sidetracked into the maths and science stream. Even at that age, I preferred economics, finance and current affairs to trigonometry and chemistry. Too often it is taken for granted that boys should concentrate on science while girls study languages. A full examination of the options would be welcomed by every youngster I've spoken to.

No longer is it assumed that every farmer's son will automatically go into farming. I do not want to speculate upon what education is for, but I do feel that study should be directed towards clearer goals, that pupils should have something more tangible to aim for than vague Highers at the end of five or six years' hard work.

Recently I attended the prize-giving ceremony at the School of Rural Studies, Clinterty. Informal discussion with several members of the board of management left me most impressed with their general attitude. Fully acknowledging that fewer people will be needed on the land in future, they have enthusiastically set out to offer their students as wide a range of courses as possible.

Responding to the call for diversification in the countryside, Clinterty is providing courses in leisure and recreation, tourism, arboriculture and many other alternative subjects, as well as the basic skills of computerisation, finance and management, which are common to all businesses.

Throughout my life I have embraced several careers, and I've always been grateful for the sound education I received at the local school. And curiously, the necessity to complete my homework quickly worked to my advantage in later years.

It stood me in good stead when I had to study such things as Treasury reports on export credit financing, or get to grips, in limited time, with balancing the budget of Grampian Region.

Without that belt on the chin from Mr Drimmie I might never have lifted my head from the neep dreels. When your nose is on a grindstone, all you see is the grindstone.

Game of hide and seek . . .

I did not like the gamie, and the gamie did not like me. I tried to avoid confrontation by keeping out of his way. The fact that he was lazy and worked a very short day helped immensely.

Maybe I misjudged him, but he was never to be seen before ten o' clock in the morning. I could have my rabbits caught and into the house by the time he came on the scene. However, I much preferred to go poaching in the evening when they were out feeding in the oat crops. My collie, Bess, had a great turn of speed. She could flick a running rabbit into the air and catch it as it was coming down.

The rabbits so badly damaged the crop in the fields round the foot of the hill that often there was bare ground for about one hundred yards. They had to cross that expanse from their feeding area to the safety of burrows in the wood. Just why our gamie objected to my weekly take of rabbits I'll never know, for he himself certainly failed to keep the menaces in check.

Sixteen rabbits twice a week plus a couple of hares, was all we needed, yet the gamie grudged me them. Rabbit meat was a regular part of our weekly meals. We had them stewed on a Tuesday and roasted on a Friday. For me, roast rabbit remains one of the tastiest dishes on the menu.

I suppose by the very nature of their job gamekeepers rarely appeared to be hurrying. Hard-pressed horsemen resented seeing the man strolling around fixing his snares. Often, he would stand still for hours waiting for a hoodie craw to appear, and country folk grudged him his leisurely pace.

One Glenlivet gamekeeper used to meet the local farmers as he passed by the smiddy. One day, he remarked that he hadn't a holiday in thirty years. "Awa ye go", came the sharp reply "fit ye mean tae say is that ye've had a thirty-year holiday".

In the early years of the war, rabbit became very popular as it provided a welcome extra to the meagre weekly ration of meat. During the early 40s, every parish had an agricultural executive committee whose task it was to increase farm food production by every means possible. Tenant farmers could appeal to the committee for help

Hamish with his collie, Shep

73

in reducing the serious waste to arable crops caused by rabbits. And so, eventually, a trapper was engaged to work our gamekeeper's beat. In the first month, he caught six thousand rabbits of marketable size. The gamie wrongly believed that we were the farmers who had approached the committee, and his resentment knew no bounds. As a direct result of the severe cull, the oat crops grew right up to the woodland fences for the first time in living memory. And the land lost its perpetual stink of rabbit droppings and urine.

But – there's aye a something. Inevitably, our weekly quota of rabbit for the pot became difficult to find. To make matters worse, my dog was getting older and stiffer and losing much of her earlier enthusiasm. Luckily, a local poacher was able to sell me a lurcher – a cross between a collie and a greyhound. My dog was young, fast and deadly. To my delight, I found I could cut rabbit-catching time by half.

There is aye somebody ready to carry tales, and the gamie soon got to hear of my dog. One morning, as I was heading towards the steading with my catch, he suddenly appeared from the stackyard and intercepted me. "Dogs like that are not for the likes of you", he shouted. Quick as a flash, he shot from the hip. "Bang" went both barrels, and my poor dog fell stone dead less than six feet from me. There was nothing I could do, and as I buried the bonny creature where he had fallen I swore vengeance on that man and all his tribe of fellow gamekeepers. From then on I carried a shotgun; and pheasant, grouse and roe deer supplemented rabbits at our lunchtimes.

Things change, though. Here in the 90s, we have a shortage of gamekeepers. The countryside could sorely do with more of them. Nature lovers deplore the current shortage of wildlife, and the RSPB claim that certain species of birds, such as lapwing and partridge, have been decimated by modern farming methods. If these people would really study the position instead of just shouting about it they would find that the scarcity is caused by the two creatures that gamekeepers waged perpetual war on – namely, the hoodie crow and the fox.

In the nesting season, hoodie crows can be seen quartering the ground quite methodically. During the course of a day they will systematically clear the eggs from ground nests of peasies and partridges. In addition, they will kill the young leverets that the mother hare has carefully hidden in a scrape. Next day they'll move on to fresh territory and wreak almost total destruction on every living creature in trees and hedges.

Foxes are not quite so systematic, but they, too, can cover vast distances. I've known them to raid the nesting sites of seabirds on the steep cliffs by the sea. Add on the destructive capacity of wild mink and of the many feral cats that now roam our countryside, and it is a wonder that we have any wildlife at all.

Maybe what we need is not a district agricultural committee nowadays, but a district wildlife committee prepared to employ gamekeepers to protect the wildlife from the wildlife. But never please never, let them shoot a young boy's dog.

Brave Jean shows the way

Jean was the bravest person I ever knew.

Either that or she was the wisest. Anyway, she had sufficient bravery or wisdom to swim against the tide.

She was one of the many customers on my evening milk round. Although there were frequent pay-offs in the Keith woollen mills where she was a darner, Jean was always kept on.

I couldn't begin accurately to estimate her take-home pay; but most certainly in that year of 1936 it must have been less than thirty shillings a week.

I well remember how I used to dread Friday nights on the milk round. That was the night we were paid for the week's deliveries, but it was also the night on which men got paid off if work was scarce.

Dole money was little more than a pittance, and the unfortunate man's wife had to prune and pare her spending to balance her weekly budget.

One of the first items to be cut was the milk bill. A reduced sale was bad, but a cancelled order was hard to bear. There were no big spenders in those days and every customer's order was precious. During the 1930s, the milk marketing board did not extend its activities much beyond a twelve mile radius of Aberdeen. Milk surplus to the requirements of our retail customers had to be turned into butter or cheese. Then, in turn, a market had to be found for these products.

Nearly twenty farmworkers were dependent for their wages on the money coming in from our two milk rounds. Virtually every pay-off in the town directly affected us as well as the man who lost his job.

Many skilled tradesmen had been out of work since 1930. Master masons, joiners and plumbers had cut their workforces to the bone. Often, there was only the boss and one apprentice. If a job turned up, he could call on men on a Saturday and they would be ready to start on Monday.

No house-building had taken place in Keith for many years. There was a severe shortage of accommodation, but the local council wouldn't borrow the money needed to remedy the situation.

Then – out of the blue – Jean announced that she was going to build a house. The whole town was agog.

How could she afford to build, she being only a working girl? "The lassie is mad", said some who didn't know her. Those who did thought different, Jean had a good head and was nobody's fool.

Whether she had read the preachings of the brilliant Canadian economist, John Maynard Keynes, I can't say. He advocated that governments and individuals should borrow money to get folk back to work.

In the US, President Franklin D. Rossevelt made a modest start to reflate the American economy by inaugurating a programme of public works.

The British Government, alas, did not follow his example. Yet the public purse could clearly get better value from building houses and roads during a slump than during a boom time.

Jean seemed to know this. Her architect received many builders' estimates for

the job. For the construction of her house, comprising two bedrooms, living-room, kitchen and bathroom, each estimate was under £300 – yes £300. The successful tender was at the incredibly low figure of £250.

I doubt if anyone made any profit on the job, but the tradesmen got back to work and it was a real labour of love to all of them. Stonemasons, joiners, painters and plumbers gladly grasped the chance to exercise skills which had been idle for too long.

The house is a credit to those who built it; and recently I saw it advertised at an asking price of £55,000. Jean lived and died a proud woman, happy in her own home.

Well, here we are in another recession. It is not, to my mind, nearly as bad as that of the hungry 1930s. Thanks to the Beveridge Plan we now have a welfare state that alleviates the very worst of the poverty. But the present recession is real enough and severe enough to those whose jobs have disappeared or whose businesses have collapsed. Certainly, the spending power of all of them goes down dramatically and that affects the retail traders.

To remain in business, most tradesmen will once again sharpen their pencils and give really competitive quotes to get the work. I know several farmers in my age group who intend to retire within the next few years. They can't decide exactly when to finish up and roup out. But one thing is sure. If they have Jean's wisdom they'll be ordering the new house for their retirement now. They will never have a better chance to get real value for money.

It is anybody's guess how farming will fare in the next few years. What with the set-aside scheme and the new sheep and cattle breeding stock guarantess to pay for, I can hardly believe that the CAP will survive for long. It hasn't achieved what it set out to do. Surpluses continue to build up at an alarming rate. Since the introduction of milk quotas nine years ago, production in Italy has shot up and they now put into intervention stores four times as much cheese as formerly.

At the present time, the Irish are buying up big bullocks from Scotland and selling the carcases into intervention because they have a larger quota in the EC than they can fill. There are probably other examples relating to such commodities as wine, olives and rape seed. Taken together, they will almost certainly bankrupt the EC budget within three years.

I just have the feeling that 1993 could be the year for bargains. With interest rates now at manageable levels this could be the time to act on that big project you have in mind.

Valued farm service over the years . . .

I needed the services of a valuator the other week.

Some time ago I erected an expensive fence around land on which I have just vacated the tenancy.

An independent assessment was called for to settle upon a price for posts and wire that was fair to both outgoer and ingoer. Farmers usually seek an expert's opinion in such matters to avoid haggling between both parties.

I haven't had word of the valuation yet, nor of the fee for the job. But I cannot help being impressed at the wisdom of our ancestors in evolving such a workable system.

Where there are lots of items to be priced – as when a whole farm tenancy is being vacated and a new man taking over – it is usual for each party to engage a valuator to work on his behalf.

Thereafter, the tenents themselves play no part in the proceedings, relying entirely on the men they appoint to see that each side gets fair play. I say "men", because to date I have not heard of women undertaking such work.

Before commencing their inspections, the two valuators agree to call on the services of a third valuator should they find themselves in serious disagreement. This third man, the oversman, plays an important role as he becomes the final aribiter, the Solomon, in all disputes.

I've taken the trouble to delve a bit deeper into the business of arbitration, and also into the wider sphere of farm valuations. It has been my great good fortune to receive on loan some extremely interesting diaries kept by two valuators of yesteryear.

From Mr Gerald Lumsden, at Huntly, I have a diary for 1894, meticulously kept by his grandfather who was farmer and valuator at Lenshie Farm, Inverkeithny. And from Mr Charles Gair, of East Moniack Farm, near Inverness, I have four beautifully-kept notebooks with immense details of valuations his father carried out in the 1930s and 1940s. The farms he officiated on stretch across the North from Moray to Sutherland.

I have had several fascinating evenings, thanks to the endeavours of these two men. Both were bonny writers of bold copperplate figuring, a fact which reflects the emphasis that was placed on the three Rs in their schooldays.

There were no calculators in those days, and their arithmetic workings are clearly shown. As well as the lists of the many farm items they dealt with at the Whitsunday and Martinmas terms, each kept a note of the wages paid to their own farm staff.

A foreman horseman in 1894 got £16 plus house and perquisites for his six months of labour. In 1934, the wage rate was £26 for the same period. The perquisites hadn't changed at all. These were four bolls of oatmeal, one load of firewood, one-and-a-half loads of potatoes, plus a further two hundred yards of potatoes on the farm which the man would plant and lift himself.

Mr Gair's notebooks show that wage rates increased dramatically during World War I but fell back rapidly in the slump of the early 1930s.

But to get back to the fascinating role of the valuators. Their task was to decide

the amount of grain a growing crop would produce, to calculate the value per running yard of the fencing on the farm, and to evaluate the dung in the heap per cubic yard.

The actual measurement of the dung heap, and the measuring of the fences, was commonly done by the local dominie. Not many perks came the way of the school-master, but measuring was one job where he excelled and his results were never queried.

Some of our older retired farmers can still remember the whole class of older boys being set to the task of measuring. Such meticulous work must have added meaning to an otherwise dull academic subject.

It was also the valuator's job to put a price on such diverse items as the corn bruiser, the threshing mill (if there was one), and the chains and sliders for tying the cattle in the byres.

Also included among tenants' fixtures were the field gates, the swey and the crook at the kitchen fire, the bedroom fires and the curtain fittings.

After their separate inspections the two valuators would get together and compare notes. Often with a bit of give and take, they would arrive at a mutually-agreed price. Where agreement could not be reached, each man would put his arguments to the oversman, whose word was final.

The more I read of these transactions of former days, the more enthusiastic I become about the whole concept of arbitration. What might have developed into bitter argument and long-lasting feuds became, instead, a well-structured pattern of negotiation. Our forebears were'na "feel", and I'm sure a lot of present-day bickering could be avoided if only we applied their lessons. Maybe, to, we could get practical solutions to political problems.

Now that I have nothing to do with party politics, lots of people of all political persuasions talk to me. I am not exaggerating when I claim that ninety per cent of all who live in Scotland want a solution to the present impasse on the constitutional question.

There is widespread frustration with the antics of those politicians who refuse to get together and come up with a programme of events which will lead to the setting up of a Parliament in Edinburgh.

Each party leaders is so imprisoned within his own narrow party philosophy that none will agree to anythmg the other side says.

To break the deadlock, let them appoint an arbiter and abide by his decision. If it was important to get an accurate, acceptable answer on the value of a dung heap, how much more important the need to find a harmonious solution to the question of how best to govern Scotland.

O' mice an' men – a toast to Robbie

Unlike Robbie Burns, I wasn't ploughing when I played havoc with a family of field mice recently.

I am rarely allowed to do tractorwork since plunging down that twenty-eight foot gully on the wee tractor a couple of years ago.

Although I made a complete recovery from my bashes, the same could not be said of the poor tractor.

Everybody has a favourite Burn's poem, and mine is *To A Mouse. Tam o' Shanter* may be racier and more flamboyant, and *The Twa Dugs* may give a fuller description of the poet's life and times, but his short poem dedicated to the moosie vividly describes both Robbie's hard life and his enduring love of nature.

When the coulter of his plough turned up a nest of field mice and destroyed their shelter on a cold November day, Robbie had only compassion for the poor wee things. I must say I felt much the same sympathy for the half-dozen mice I disturbed in December.

We find that the white glazed redundant kitchen sinks make perfect receptacles for feeding minerals to our cattle. A puckle coos barging about can easily cowp a plastic container, scattering its expensive powdered contents. The solid old kitchen sink, though, can withstand a good daily buffeting.

We had been shifting the bulling heifers to their winter quarters among the whin bushes, so I got the Land Rover into four-wheel-drive and crossed the grass field to where the sink was lying. It was upside down and, mindful of its weight, I started to turn it over by tipping up one end. There, inside, was a beautifully-constructed sphere, almost the size of a football.

It was perfectly rounded and looked at first glance like a piece of the intricate basketwork you can see at craft fairs. However, on closer inspection, I discovered that the material was not cane, and not even straw. The sphere consisted entirely of barley yavins, or awns.

Each yavin, measuring roughly three inches was laid parallel to its neighbour and fixed at both ends by other yavins laid at a different angle. What really intrigued me was the fact that the angle was about forty-five degrees – not at right angles as you might expect.

Six fat, shiny mice scurried away into the long grass round the sink. I was eager to look for an entrance to the sphere, but sadly my dog made a swift dive at the structure and broke it. The wind quickly got hold of the light yavins and scattered them.

In the sixth verse of his poem Burn's writes:

That wee bit heap o' leaves an' stibble
Has cost thee mony a weary nibble!

The structure I saw, however, was no heap. It was a carefully woven nest of material which had been painstakingly selected for length.

Moreoever, from its bright golden colour I jaloused that the yavins had been gathered and the house built before the barley was harvested. Last year's wet hairst gave much of the barley straw a weathered look.

Besides, yavins that have been through a combine's drum and along the straw walkers end up about half-an-inch long or even less. How else would they manage to get into your belly button and jab you? The yavins used by the mice were shiny and totally unblemished. If they'd been left undisturbed in the upturned sink, they would likely have kept their colour and shape.

The barley field was fifteen feet away from the sink. So each tiny spear had been carried through an undergound tunnel. I did notice that there was no spare material lying around.

Thy wee bit housie, too, in ruin!
Its silly wa's the win's are strewin'!
An' naething now, to big a new ane
O' foggage green!
An' bleak December's winds ensuin'
Baith snell an' keen!

Okay, so mice are mice and can be a blasted nuisance about any farm Nevertheless, I did feel sorry for these poor orphans. They had the foresight to build a home in that cosy cavern to see them through the winter. All that I could do for them that day was to quote still more of Robbie's poem:

But, Mousie, thou art no thy lane
In proving foresight may be vain:
The best laid schemes o' mice an' men
Gang aft agley,
An' lea'e us nought but grief an' pain
For promis'd joy.

In the last verse of that lovely poem the sympathy of the reader swings back to the poet:

Still thou are blest compar'd wi' me
The present only toucheth thee:
But oh! I backward cast~ my e'e
On prospects drear!
An' forward tho' I canna see
I guess an' fear!

That is powerful stuff and portrays very clearly the trials and tribulations of Robbie Burns' life as a farmer. I can't claim to have endured such hardship I'm glad to say. Certainly, I have worked hard and put in long hours in my lifetime, but I've always enjoyed what I was doing and I would do it all again.

And I like looking forward to the next sale, the next calf, the next crop, the next day, the next year and, I hope, the next century.

Whether it relates to mice or polar bears, white rhinos or the rare creatures in a Brazilian rainforest, I go back to the second verse of Robbie's poem – back to what I consider are probably the six finest lines of poetry in the Engish language:

I'm truly sorry man's dominion
Has broken Nature's social union
An' justifies that ill opinion
Which makes thee startle
At me, they poor earth--born companion,
An' fellow-mortal!

Escape from milk float and watery end

I've been heart sorry for the folk of Tayside these past weeks.

To see them struggling in a losing battle with the rising waters makes me thankful that I farm in a part of the world where "we neither drucht nor droon".

Even in a severe spate, our burns mostly stay within their own watercourse. From source to sea, they are only a few miles long. The River Tay, on the other hand, draws water from a huge area of Scotland.

If the snow melts rapidly over a wide acreage of farmland and hillside the natural riverbed just can't cope. I have twice experienced – quite dramatically – the power of flooded burns, and I'm lucky to be alive to tell the tale.

When I was twelve, I was dispatched one spring afternoon to deliver a young calf to a croft in the Glen of Newmill. The only shelt available was little Donald, a gurky wee garron about thirteen hands high.

Donald was no speedster and had already been out on the milk round for five hours. My departure was delayed for an hour while he had his feed.

Knowing that the Garrelburn was in spate, I went by Grange, adding at least two miles to a journey that was maybe five miles. The flat milk cart had only me as driver and a box of straw containing the calf, which was firmly sewn into a hessian sack.

Animal-welfare rights enthusiasts frown on the practice of transporting calves in sacks, but it was common practice in pre-war days. During the war, I can recall arriving home on leave on a heavily-overcrowded train.

In the guard's van – the only place you could get room to move – there were thirty calves from English farms, all bound for the North-east.

None of them were in any way distressed within their canvas shrouds. At Aberdeen Joint Station they were placed on open porters' trolleys and loaded onto the various trains that ran to all parts of the North-east before Dr Beeching took his axe to the branch lines.

I must have taken three hours to cover the seven miles that afternoon, and it rained non-stop. The croft was high up on the glen, giving me a panoramic view not only of the road I had come but also of the much, much shorter route I could take if only I could cross the burn. The older crofter advised me to risk the ford as the water had receded slightly.

Horses always know when they are headed for home, and Donald showed no fear in plunging into the water. Soon, he was immersed halfway up his belly, and still we hadn't reached the proper bed of the ford. The light, rubber-tyred milk cart eventually began to float.

Before Donald could reach the centre of the twenty yard flood he had lost footing and was swimming. The raging current was stronger than the horse, and soon we were all floating downstream. Donald's front feet were scrambling on the far side of the ford, but he wasn't able to counteract the sideways pull of the water.

The box of straw floated off the cart as I clambered along the left shaft and, with the reins in my hand, made a jump for the bank of the burn. I tied the reins to a fence post, then waded back into the water and grabbed the pony's collar.

As I heaved, I seemed to give the poor beast extra courage. He found a fresh footing and with a determined scramble, got all four feet on the wide of the ford, enabling himself to pull harder than the sideways pull of the water.

The whole episode was over in less than two minutes. If you were to see the Garrelburn on a summer's day, complete with the concrete bridge that has replaced the ford, it would be difficult to imagine how near the sheltie and I came to being swept away.

A rapid thaw and continued heavy rain – the disastrous combination that has caused such havoc in Perthshire – once nearly cost me my life. The winter of 1964 had been a long one, and by February the sheep were very hungry.

Unable to scrape down through the depth of snow cover, they were totally dependent on hay and silage forked daily from a tractor trailer. For handiness, we had brought the flock near the steading, to a field that had a burn running along the bottom, parallel to the public road. That year, the burn was completely bridged over by drifted snow.

One Friday the rain came down on top of ice and the treacherous conditions immobilised our tractors. As a result, the sheep were nearly three hours late in being fed.

A neighbour's tractor went up the public road; and, just as Pavlov's dogs responded to a bell being rung, so my sheep rushed towards the passing tractor. The snow bridge over the burn collapsed, and the flock went tumbling in.

I was just about to start the afternoon milking when I noticed what was happening. Dropping my milking machines, I rushed to the burn and jumped straight in through the snow bridge. The freezing water reached to my chest but I didn't notice. A sheep bumped against my chest and I threw it to the bank. Then came another, and another, and another. My cattleman – who was in his sixties – grabbed them from me and dragged them up the bank. Soon, the weight of sheep against my chest was almost overwhelming, but thankfully my two tractormen arrived on the scene. One jumped in to help me while the other dragged the sheep away. All four of us were given superhuman strength that afternoon.

Every sheep that we snatched from the water recovered. Out of a total of one hundred and ninety-six we saved all but nine. But for our foolhardy action, we would have lost the lot because there was no sloping bank where they could reach and the burn was running with tremendous force.

That was the winter I made up my mind to search for a farm near the sea.

Punch-drunk and miraculous cure . . .

The mild spring-like weather we've enjoyed on the Moray coast this past week is really unseasonable.

I've even seen bats flying about on several evenings. Don't get me wrong. I have enjoyed every minute of the sunny days; but in mid-February we ought to have frost. The lack of it will mean a carry-over of diseases in our winter wheat and barley crops.

I went into the garden for some leeks and found the ground so dry that I dug over a bit ready for early tatties when I decide to plant them.

Two tiny potatoes that had been missed at lifting had healthy sprouts about an inch long. Then, coming across the shell of what had been a lovely Kerrs Pink, my mind turned back to an old friend.

Willie was my good friend and also my banker. As a friend he was kind, cheery, hospitable and exceptionally generous. As a banker he was none of these, in fact, he was a pest.

Willie knew perfectly well that my milk cheque was paid straight through to the bank on the 17th of each month, yet he would phone me on the 16th to ask if I had any money coming in. Overdraft facilities were practically unobtainable, despite the fact that I owned my farm with only a modest mortgage.

Things got so bad that I had to say to him: "Now look here! I was with this bank long before you came and I intend being with this bank long after you have gone, so you'll just have to learn to put up with me for as long as you are here".

Out of banking hours, all that was forgotten. We were frequent visitors to each others' houses. Willie's wife was every bit as friendly as he was. She was the perfect hostess because you could see that she thoroughly enjoyed having folk in for a meal and a blether.

They would have made wonderful parents, but, sadly, they had no children. Willie was just o'er canny. When they married, he was too poor to start a family. Then the war came and that was no time to have a family. Later, they lived in a Glasgow flat – and that was no place to rear a family.

Finally, when conditions were right, no family appeared. They had left it too late. Occasionally, when he'd had a few drams, Willie would tell me how he envied me my three children. "When I go", he'd continue, "I'll gang aff the earth like a rotten tattie. And fit maks it a' the waur tae thole is that it's a' my ain fault".

Well, Willie is awa, but he left me lovely memories. His comments about the rotten tattie made me think a lot about his life and my own, and it changed our relationship as banker and customer.

Sometimes we would meet up at social events. On one memorable occasion we were both to attend the annual dance of a neighbouring farmers club.

Selling us the tickets the club president kindly asked us to come by his house for a drink before the function started.

Willie stuck to his customary single glass of whisky, but I would be bolder and accepted a glass of homemade punch. It tasted very pleasant so I had another half glass, all in the space of about thirty minutes.

There was a little trace of alcohol in the punch and I never found out what its base consisted of. Maybe it was clear whisky; but from its effect, I suspect it was a mixture of gin and vodka.

During the ten minutes it took to reach the hall I began to feel fairly woozy. By the time I'd hung my coat in the clockroom I was decidedly squiffy. When the hall started to reel – and that without the Eightsome – I reckoned I'd better get home quickly.

Good friend that he was, Willie

immediately consented to drive me. He arranged with another friend to drive his car the fourteen miles to my farm while he drove mine. By the end of the twenty minute journey I was flat our on the back seat. Willie roused me and asked me if he'd help to see me to bed. I thanked him, but said I had to see a cow before I went to my bed.

"Ye're in nae condition tae see ony coo", said Willie. "Please gang awa back tae the dance", I told him, "I must see this coo". "Then we'll help ye", they both volunteered – although neither came from a farming background.

I took off my dancing shoes, my sporran and my Prince Charlie jacket, protected my kilt with a khaki overall, got into my wellies and staggered to the byre. Sure enough, just as I had expected, the recently-calved cow was stretched out in her stall with all the classic symptoms of milk fever. She looked quite dead but her pulse was still fairly strong.

I fetched the bottle of calcium and the flutter valve from the medicine cupboard. Getting the hollow needle into a cow's neck vein is difficult enough when you are sober . . . Anyway, thanks to long practice, I eventually succeeded and let half the contents of the bottle slowly drain under the skin.

At that stage I was standing upright and managing to remain steady enough. But when I bent over the cow to reach for the milk vien, close by the udder, I kept losing my balance.

"The Muckin o' Geordie's Byre has naething on you the nicht", laughed Willie. A spurt of blood through the needle told me I had found the right spot, and I let all the calcium trickle in slowly. Well, anyone who has ever seen the process will know that the cure is almost miraculous. It's about the equivalent of raising Lazarus from the dead.

My patient rolled her eyes, shook her lugs, then lifted her head. She shochled a few times until she got into a sitting position, then staggered to her feet and began to drink from her water bowl as if nothing had happened. She was completely cured. I didn't see Willie again for about four months – not until I went to ask for an overdraft to buy my wintering lambs.

He sat behind his desk with a broad smile on his face. "Fairly that, Hamish", he said. "Any beggar that wis as sozzled as you were yon nicht and could still pey attention tae his work can easily have my bank's money".

Yowes will miss our stalwart Bob

Bob won't be doing the lambing this year.

The four hundred and fifty yowes are all there, looking fit and due to start lambing in the first week of April.

Although officially retired, Bob normally would have been taking his stint in the big, airy shed, watching out for signs of a ewe starting to lamb.

She would be corralled with two hurdles in a corner of the pen and allowed to get on with it. Bob would intervene only if there were complications.

I have always considered Bob Robertson, of Corskellie Farm, Rothiemay, to be a real master when it comes to sheep. I know that his organisational ability is second to none.

Corskellie has long held a fascination for me because the land is unbelievably straight – that is, steep. You can see Corskellie on the far bank of the River Deveron, rising steeply from the river to a height of 750ft at the top, as you drive along the narrow, winding and picturesque road from Bridge of Marnoch to Rothiemay.

There is just enough flat land to hold the steading for the cattle. And now a space has been gouged out for the commodious sheep shed.

Corskellie was famed for fully fifty years for the quality of its half-bred lambs. These were in great demand from English buyers and they regularly topped the September ewe lamb sales in Aberdeen.

Every August, Bob – and his father before him – would buy the best Cheviot gimmers in Caithness to add replacements to Corskellie's flock of big, able yowes.

Then, top Border Leicester rams would be bought to produce the famous half-bred offspring.

But times change. In the relentless search for greater efficiency and greater production, the status of the Cheviot has been downgraded.

For one thing, there was the problem of the breed's relatively low prolificacy. The Robertsons could not get above one hundred and fifty per cent lambing, no matter how they tried.

Moreover, the Cheviot ewe did not take kindly to the intensive regime of a sheep shed. Even if clipped in December, she would not have regrown sufficient wool to withstand the cold winds that blow on those exposed braes in April.

So the shed is now full of bonny, brown-faced mule ewes from the North of England. These females are the progeny of Swaledale ewes and a blue-faced Leicester tup. For the past two years, lambing has exceeded two hundred per cent and this year augurs even better

The 450 ewes were X-rayed last week and one hundred and sixty-three were seen to be carrying triplets. Most will survive since they were indoors away from the icy winds and the ewes that drop single lambs will be held in the adopters to have a triplet fostered on.

The aim is to have every ewe going to grass with at least two lambs at foot. I called last week to see Bob senior, who suffered a fairly severe stroke a few days before Christmas. It just crept up on him one lunchtime while he was opening the Christmas mail and it has affected one side and one leg.

Thanks to the excellent medical care provided at Foresterhill and now at Huntly hospital, he is making a slow but steady recovery.

He's full of praise for the physiotherapists who put him through a daily routine of exercises. But, for this year at least, he will be cared for by Margaret, his extremely capable wife, instead of caring for lambing ewes.

I have a particular liking for the Robertsons of Corskellie for two good reasons. First, I greatly admire their tenacity in building a highly-successful farming enterprise from such inhospitable conditions.

In virtually every country I have visited in my travels, only the flat land is cultivated. Steep terrain is left in virgin bush or planted with trees. Here in the North-east, we farmers cultivate land that no other country would tackle.

Now, there are certainly plenty of other farms with straight parks. But Corskellie is all straight. Bob was telling me that when he started full-time on the farm after leaving school at fourteen, nothing but the young, fittest horses could get the loaded neep cairts off these perpendicular braes.

His son, Robert junior, stresses that four-wheel-drive tractors are a tremendous boon and have a far better safety record than the two-wheel-drive versions.

My second reason for maintaining a soft spot for Corskellie is that both my daughter Lorna and my son Michael received excellent grounding in stockmanship there.

Every vet student has to gain experience lambing sheep; but the two seasons with Bob Robertson's Cheviots gave Lorna such a liking for the job that she went on to assist with lambing blackfaces at Keithmore, near Dufftown, and then with a flock of eight hundred crosses on the Scottish/English border.

When lambing is in full swing, nobody gets time off, and Lorna came home on a Saturday evening only for fresh clothes. Her entire conversation centred on this yowe and that yowe, this loss and that success.

"You know, dad", she said, "if I could lamb yowes all the year round, I wouldn't bother going back to vet college".

It all paid off for her when she took up her first post as a vet in Newcastle. During her very first lambing season, the senior partner would seek to allay the fears of a worried farmer on the other end of the telephone.

"A stuck ewe, is it? Right. I'll send our expert out right away. Here, Lorna", he'd say, handing over the phone. "Take down the directions yourself".

My son, Michael, completed a BA business-management degree at Robert Gordons and set off for the financial world in London. As a student, he did one lambing at Corskellie, just for the money. All students are hard up and he didn't flinch at the prospect of three weeks of long hours with no chance to spend any of the wages.

The following spring, when he no longer needed the money, there he was back among the Corskellie yowes. He had saved up his holiday entitlement to have three weeks at the lambing. That year, it poured every day and he never got his oilskins off.

Yet when it was over and he had returned to London, he decided that his future lay with livestock. Now he is the farmer and I am the gofer – go for this and go for that.

Stormy term of office

We had a lively question-and-answer session the other week at the Rhynie Farmers' Discussion Group. The questions were many and varied.

Some of the younger members of the audience were keen to learn more about working a farm with horses. Others wanted to know which of all the inventions and changes I'd seen in my lifetime had impressed me most.

It was difficult to be specific on that question because there have been so many big changes.

The combine harvester certainly comes high on my list of major improvements. Before its introduction, sheaves had to be forked here and there half-a-dozen times before being threshed and finally secured in sacks for sale. It was year round drudgery.

The coming of electricity, with its many applications in farmhouse and steading, also represents an enormous change. Then again, without the introduction of antibiotics I would probably have died of septicaemia from my several injuries over the years.

Another vast improvement has been in the field of hygiene. Thanks to modern detergents and the advent of refrigeration, milk now has a shelf life of half-a-week, whereas it used to be half a-day when I was a youngster.

The question that intrigued me most, however, was: why did I never speak of my term as rector of Aberdeen University? I hastened to assure the questioner that I frequently refer to that wonderful experience, but usually when I am speaking to non-farming audiences.

In the short time available – for the evening was wearing late – I explained that it had fallen to my lot to be elected rector during one of the toughest crises in the five hundred year history of the university.

In 1985, the year of my election, the university was facing a deficit on the year's working of £1.25 million. The projections for the following years were even worse

Something drastic had to done. Tough decisions were needed. Howls of protest went up from some sections of the student body and from many of the staff whose jobs were at risk.

These protests were listened to and evaluated, but most often they could not be allowed to affect the harsh decisions to lop many jobs and close some departments.

A lesser man than Principal George McNicol might have bowed under the immense pressure, and I regard it a privilege to have been in a position to help get the right decisions taken by the University Court.

Sometimes the voting was perilously close, and had I voted the way the students wanted me to vote the university would still be stumbling from crisis to crisis. The strong left-wing element in the National Union of Students believed that it was the duty of the Government to pour in money to meet every deficit. This organised group sought confrontation at every opportunity.

Now, throughout my farming career I had never taken part in protest marches by farmers against unfair measures by successive Governments, and there was no way that I was prepared to lead protest marches by students.

I was brought up on a farm in the 1930s and early 1940s where one worked a long day, every day. When I won an RAF scholarship to St Andrews University for the autumn of 1943, I thought I was in heaven.

Daily from Monday to Saturday, we RAF cadets had to rise at 6.30 and put in ninety minutes physical training. We attended three hours of standard student lectures in the forenoons and the afternoons were devoted to four hours of RAF training. We had Saturday afternoon and all day Sunday to ourselves. After the never ending grind of farm work it felt like easy street.

I regarded the regular students as leading the life of Reilly. I thought then that students were a privileged sector of society, and I think it yet. The university system and the student body get a big share of taxpayers' money. I don't grudge them one penny, and in all my public life I have striven to make university education available to everyone who can benefit from it.

However, I have always believed that the taxpayers' money should be spent wisely and that education establishments should be run efficiently To my mind, the situation within Aberdeen University in 1985 satisfied neither of these requirements. For instance, in the theology department professors and lecturers outnumbered students. It was much the same in the Greek and Hebrew faculties and in several other cases, student numbers were just too low to justify the existence of the department.

It never ceases to amaze me that some students and academics think their industry should be immune from cuts and changes. There isn't a manufacturing or service industry in Britain that hasn't had to face radical change, and redundancies are a harsh fact of life in all sectors.

Votes of no confidence on the principal and on myself by small groups of students caused us no loss of sleep. The changes went through, and today the university is solvent and can look forward to the next century with confidence.

The lecturing staff have been reduced by about thirty per cent, yet student intake had gone up by twelve per cent. And although the ratio of staff to students has risen from eight to one to fourteen to one, there has been an increase of ten per cent in the award of first class honours degrees.

What pleases me most about the changes is the impetus they have given to a steady increase in the number of mature students. With new access courses and flexibility in assessing incoming students, anyone capable of proving that he or she can benefit from university education will be considered for entry.

I get encouraged when I hear of farmers in their thirties deciding to take a university course. If they would study subjects such as ecology and chemistry or environmental science we farmers might, in due course, get knowledgeable officials coming round telling us what to do. If we must have officials breathing down our nesks, let's breed our own.

Of course, I could have wished for an easier passage during my time as rector, and I envy my successors. But I am proud to realise that the changes I helped to push through will benefit the university and its students long after those who instigated them are forgotten.

Reaping rewards of livestock bonanza

I've never had much luck at the one-armed bandit. Fruit machines are not my forte.

The latest don't even have handles. You just press a button and the cherries, oranges, pineapples and bells go whizzing round. A winning line of three matching images just doesn't appear when I'm around, so I gave up donating coins to such machines years ago.

A jackpot is something that happens to other people. I have always had to work for any money I got, and at times I've worked hard for dashed little. Many of the posts I have held in public life and in politics have been unpaid. In some cases, not even expenses were reimbursed.

But now, for the first time, things have changed. This spring every farm product has been in great demand. I have been coming home from market with prices that have exceeded even my most optimistic forecasts.

With the mild winter we've experienced here on the coast, the Cheviot lambs have fattened earlier than usual. Each draw of the five hundred flock went to market a month early; and at every sale, the prices were higher than we'd expected. We came home well pleased with the margin between buying price and selling price. If we had sold them a month later we would have had an even larger margin. Undoubtedly, there must be some feeders who have managed to sell at double their buying price.

My mother used to have a saying: "If ifs and ands were pots and pans there would be no need for tinkers". So – I'll content myself and admit that the sheep have done us well this winter in spite of all the doubts and misgivings we had in the autumn.

Thanks to the devaluation of the pound following upon Black Wednesday, the French and German buyers have been prepared to pay us more pounds for our animals. This means the cattle trade is also booming. Prices for store cattle have gone through the roof.

As usual, we have far more young stock than we can provide grazing for, so lot after lot of bullocks and heifers have gone through the sale rings at Thainstone market. All have fetched prices in excess of expectation. We used to be delighted with 120p per kg for bullocks, but this spring returns have jumped to 140-150p. Luckily, there are still plenty of cattle to go from our courts between now and May, when the grass really grows.

I noticed in the press this week that the inventor of Parkinson's Law had died. In the 1950s he propounded the principle that "a job expands to fill the time available for its completion". Well, I have a similar theory with wintering cattle, the stirks expand to fill the court space available to them.

When the courts are filled in October there is room at the feed barrier for all the beasts. By mid January, they are jostling for trough room and the biggest ones have to be sold off to make space. From mid-January until turning-out time the same phenomenon recurs regularly. Cattle on a self-feed regime just keep expanding until they reach a state where they are attractive to buyers, who will put them on to a rapidly finishing feed regime.

Over-stocking the farm is a crime to which I must plead guilty, but this year it has fairly paid off. We have managed to send a consignment of cows and heifers to each of the monthly dairy sales since December. To say we've been pleased with the prices would be putting it mildly.

A spate of cows, both beef and dairy, have been calving lately and my son, Michael, has had to rise at least once every night for the past three weeks to check on calvers. To ease numbers, I took young calves to Thainstone last week and got prices at least £30 per head higher than I would have had the nerve to ask at home. And that was after paying the floating and sale commission. Our Simmental bull throws great growthy calves with plenty of bone and he has done us proud.

For the first time for many years the banker can have some of his money back. After four pretty grim years of crippling interest rates on borrowed capital, and low prices for our stock year after year, it is great to enjoy a bonanza – even if it may be shortlived. Those who have stuck by livestock farming are at last reaping a benefit from long hours of dedicated attention to their animals.

Economists have consistently calculated that the financial reward for the conscientious livestock farmer is less than £1 an hour. This is pathetically low when compared to the hourly rates in manufacturing industry.

I constantly marvel at the difference in the level of attention given to British and East European livestock. At the back end of last year a party of about forty Russian agriculturalists paid a three month visit to Scotland. These Russians just could not begin to understand the work ethic of either Scottish farmers or Scottish farmworkers.

For example, they couldn't believe that the same man would do both the morning and the evening milking on a dairy farm. In Russia, there would be two shifts. The idea of working on after the usual stopping time just to finish the job seemed crazy in their eyes.

The night before the group were due to return to Moscow, one young man declared that if privatising Russian agriculture resulted in his having to work as hard as the Scots do, then he for one would be changing his job. Now, I must ask the big question: who are the fools – them or us?

Does the present price bonanza we farmers are enjoying really compensate for the four harrowing years we've just come through? And remember, quite a few farmers have had to sell up.

And does it make sense to work so hard to pay Income Tax to finance the three million unemployed in our society? Or should the able bodie among that three million be helping us on the farms and sharing in our drudgery?

Tinkering with pots and pans

I really must apologise to some of the younger readers of this column – aye, and to some of the not-so-young.

It is about that quotation of my mother's: "If 'ifs' and 'ands' were pots and pans there would be no need for tinkers".

What this means, in essence, is that if there were a profusion of pots and pans there would be no need for tinkers to come and mend them. In using the quotation, I should have paused and asked myself: when last did anyone see a tinker mending pans? The answer must be about fifty years ago.

In the 1930s aluminium pans were becoming fashionable as the old open fires and ranges gave way to the Aga, Esse and Rayburn cookers.

Then, in 1940 and 1941, appeals from the Ministry of Supply saw most of the aluminium pans melted down. They were reshaped as aeroplane parts in the country's desperate scramble to find raw materials for the war effort.

Looking back from the 1990s, where the philosophy is every man for himself, it's difficult to understand and to appreciate the communal spirit of those wartime days. If there were cynics around I certainly never met any. Everyone gave freely of their time, their money, their possessions and even their lives in the battle against the common enemy.

Anyway, away went the aluminium pans and out came the old iron ones. This meant that the tinker with his blowtorch and soldering bolt was welcome at many a door where previously he had been spurned.

On our farm we had milk cans with taps and measuring cans, all of them made of tin. Being in daily use, these utensils needed frequent repairs. We normally asked the local plumber to mend the leaks.

Often, the job would be given to the newest apprentice and the resultant heap of solder was not a pretty sight. So – a visit from a tinker was always welcome. For a time at least, our milk cans would be leak-free and smooth.

I remember one elderly tinker and his wife travelling around on a flat cart drawn by a piebald shelt, and with a skewbald yearling colt tied behind. The piebald was black and white and the skewbald brown and black with some white patches. It was strange how tinkers and gypsies were attracted to the mixed colours, whereas farmers preferred animals of one predominant colour.

This particular tinker's wife was an absolute expert at basket weaving. She deftly repaired the cane baskets used for collecting eggs; and she could make a tatty old clothes basket, seemingly on its last legs, as good as new. Mostly she would round her visit off by selling us a fancy, brand new shopping basket.

Before the arrival of plastic buckets we had to repair a hole in an iron bucket with a pot mender. You bought six of these on a card from the ironmonger. The pot mender was a rare invention, consisting of several fiky parts. First, there was a thin metal washer which went on the inside of the bucket.

A bolt fitting into the centre of the washer was then pushed through the offending hole, then a cork washer was placed on the outside, followed by another thin tin washer. Finally, a small bolt was threaded onto the screw and the whole lot tightened until the hole was plugged. I still teach my grandchildren to sing and act out the old song: "There's a hole in the bucket, dear Liza, dear Liza". But it must be difficult for them to comprehend how anybody could mend a hole in a bucket with cement – as we whiles did when we had metal buckets around the farm. We truly lived in an era where we threw virtually nothing away.

Times are forever changing though; and just as the tinkers have disappeared from our ken, so the miners may well go the same way in an even shorter timespan.

The Government's reprieve for twelve closure-threatened pits is just a postponement of the inevitable. So much gas and oil has been found round our shores that these fuels are bound to undercut coal in the energy market. Open-cast coal will continue to compete for a few years, but deep-mined coal, with its high labour costs, will become a thing of the past.

But now I must tell you about something that happened on the farm last week. You know how I am aye going on about farm work teaching men to use their own initiative? Well, here's a fine example from Ian, the tractorman.

Ian was sent some miles away for a load of neeps. When he had finished loading the four tons or so of swedes he noticed that one of the tyres of the bogie was dangerously soft. He drew in to the nearest motor service station only to find that the air machine required a 10p coin to operate it – and his pockets were empty.

Always resourceful, Ian choose a nicely-shaped neep from the load and offered it to a passing housewife for 10p. "A neep for 10p? That's a bargain nooadays" replied his customer, willingly handing over the coin.

"Nae as big a bargain as my boss will get if your 10p saves his £60 tyre", said Ian as he put the air machine to work.

When you're worse for wear . . .

"Here's you, and me nae dressed."

It was just a short statement but one that was capable of lots of interpretations.

Don't worry! I'm not about to add a sexy scandal to my column, as soap serials have to do on TV nowadays to keep their viewing audience. I am merely repeating the words of my elderly neighbour when I went to pick him up for a trip to Thainstone market the other day.

As soon as he said it I burst out laughing for I hadn't heard the saying for forty years or more. In pre-war days, most housewives wore old clothes when tackling the housework in the morning. Then they made a point of "dressing" –changing into smarter and cleaner clothes for the afternoon and evening. If a visitor appeared at the door before tbe lady was "dressed", she would be black affronted.

Looking back from the present day when all but the very poorest in our society have several changes of clothes it is difficult to remember just how few garments we had.

Yet we didn't consider ourselves to be poor. We had one set of working clothes and another set for best. I hated my best suit because it was made from hairy tweed, the colour of a rusty boiler – my roosty-biler suit.

Similarly, women in those days might have only two dresses and two pairs of stockings made of either wool or lisle. Only wealthy women owned silk stockings. There were no nylons in pre war days – they hadn't been invented.

Nylon stockings, not tights, first appeared from America about 1943 brought back by sailors who had survived the Atlantic convoys. In the following year the GIs arrived bearing gifts of nylons for the girls they wanted to impress.

But the average housewife had to wait until the early l950s before nylons were readily available at prices folk could afford.

The working clothes worn in the mornings were decidedly shabby and even holey. My motber used to say that a hole was the sign of an accident, a patch was the sign of poverty. There were no comfortable slacks or shellsuits for my mother, my sisters or our two maids to slip into. Indeed, no women wore trousers, either for work or for best.

Anyway, the housework was hard and grubby in those days before washing machines, hoovers and dishwashers. Before she could even start to make the porridge the kitchen maid had to remove the previous day's ashes and reset and kindle the big open fire.

Then the fire surround and the binks at the side had to be black-leaded and polished. Later in the morning, the paraffin lamps needed to be filled and burnished. That done, the linoleum had to be polished and the rugs shaken and beaten outside.

Our big kitchen didn't even have linoleum. My earliest recollection is that it was covered by big Caithness flagstones. These were later lifted and replaced by a smooth cement surface that had to be washed every day, bar Sunday. Cleaning the black, sooty pots and pans was one of the filthy jobs that made clothes really dirty, so old garments were the order of the day in virtually every household.

Only regular callers, such as the postie and delivery men, like the milkman, the butcher, the baker and the grocer, were expected throughout the morning. Visiting by friends was confined to the afternoons. Occasionally, if there was someone to look after the children, evening visits were made.

Plenty houses lacked bathrooms and constant hot water so getting washed and "dressed" – or "riggit", or "shiftit" – all took time. If any caller came to the door much before 2.30pm they might well catch the lady of the house "nae dressed".

I remember my mother engaging a housemaid who had previously worked at a big house. The minute the dinner dishes were washed, Flora would disappear to her room and emerge later in the uniform of black dress, black stockings, white frilly apron and head-dress, ready to receive visitors at the door.

Whether my mother was expecting visitors or not was of no consequence. Flora just couldn't bear to think that someone might come to the door and see her "not dressed".

To meet the needs of our large household pancakes, girdle scones or oven scones were baked every afternoon. Flora would don a "peenie" over her uniform, turn up her cuffs and get stuck into the baking. Whichever of us school bairns got home first was rewarded with the chance to scrape the baking bowl.

Fancy baking to fill the tins took place on at least one afternoon every week, whether or not visitors were expected. Sponges, rock cakes, queen cakes, shortbread, sair heidies and other delicacies were turned out from the temperamental old paraffin oven in the pantry.

This would be one time when a little lad didn't go outside, preferring to hang around and offer to lend a hand. Many a finger I caught in the revolving spokes of the whisk before I got the hang of the thing. But it was well worth it because after use the whisk had to be licked clean.

My special favourite was the rock-cake mixture. I enjoyed it uncooked just as much as when baked. I can feel the fizz of the cream of tartar in my mouth even now.

I often think back and shudder at the amount of work these two lassies, the kitchen maid and the housemaid, had to do on our farm. There were ten folk in the farmhouse and seven men in the bothy, all of whom had to be fed three meals daily. Beside all that, my father's evening retail milk round meant that the lassies had to go to the dairy at 8.30pm and do an hour's washing of bottles and pails all by hand. The maids had two evenings off each week, when my mother and sisters tackled the dairy chores.

It is a strange thing, though, that despite all the hard work and drudgery of those days there was more visiting among friends and relations than is the case nowadays. Today, you have to worry about whether you'll interrupt your hosts' viewing of their TV programme. But a few decades ago, your only concern was that you would arrive too early and be met by the greeting: "Here's you, and me nae dressed".

Taking road to the Isles . . .

From Buckie to Bute and back all in one day seems to me to be a fair day's work.

Dispersal sales of dairy herds are very rare events nowadays. It is almost a year since I managed to buy some nice young cows at a farm dispersal sale at Beattock. I got some in Wigtownshire last November, but the sale in Bute is the only one to have taken place in Scotland this year.

Like many other dairy farmers we have been using beef bulls on our cows too extensively in the past four years, and now we have too few Friesian heifers in the pipeline to keep the milking herd up to strength. We therefore welcome the chance to procure cattle at a dispersal sale because there you are being offered a chance to buy the animals that the farmer has retained. You know that these beasts have never been put forward for sale before. By contrast, those offered at a collective sale are the ones the farmers chose to get rid of.

As well as a good selection of young Friesian cows the retiring farmer had on offer some Friesian cross Hereford bulling heifers. This cross is the most popular animal for beef herd replacements and we like to have twenty or so for sale each spring. As very few farmers now use Hereford bulls, this cross may well become unobtainable in a few years, but in the meantime we will continue to search them out.

With a 4.20am start, my son Michael, took the first stint of driving up the A95 to Aviemore. Both he and I can sleep soundly in a car, so we change drivers at seventy minute intervals. This gave me all of the Aviemore to Perth section and I had a great run.

Daylight was just about breaking on the Drumochter Summit when I saw the antlers and heads of two big stags silhouetted against the sky. The magnificent beasts were within 30 yards of the road and they made no attempt to move away. There were probably more deer close at hand, but as I was driving at motorway speed I had no chance to linger and look.

On the return journey in the evening there was sufficient light to allow us to observe three moderately large herds of hinds. They seemed to be fairly fat and to have wintered well.

We got through Glasgow before the worst of the morning rush hour traffic and arrived at Wemyss Bay just in time to catch an earlier ferry than we had planned for. On the rear window of the pick-up truck in front of us a sticker proclaimed: "A bad day's fishing is better than a good day's work".

The rain that had threatened all morning started to come down in earnest and restricted our view of the Clyde estuary. But the bacon and fried egg sandwiches which I had carefully prepared before leaving were still warming in their cooking-foil wrappers and tasted delicious.

Before anybody gives me a row for knocking my cholesterol level sky-high, let me hasten to add that the bacon was grilled the fat trimmed off and the softies were wholemeal. We didn't have anything further to eat until we stopped for a one-course meal at Balinluig on the way home.

In the past I have often attended political party conferences at Rothesay, but going this time for purely farming business heightened my anticipation. Farmers are honest and pleasant chiels when compared to politicians.

Arriving early at the farm, the two of us had ample time to study the cattle carefully and decide which to bid for and how much to pay. Then we found we had ninety minutes in hand before the auctioneer would get round to selling the cows. The rain had eased, so we took the chance to drive round most of the island. The views were spectacular. The land is well farmed – apart, that is, from the set-aside fields – and grows good grass. However, their spring has been so wet that most of the spring barley is still in the bag instead of in the ground, and this in the third week of April.

The water was standing in every furrow and the land will need a lot of fine days to dry out. What a boon these all-terrain vehicles are for the sheep farmers on the steeper farms.

The cows sold exceptionally well, with Ayrshires fetching £1,000 and freshly-calved Friesians going for as high as £2,400. When that particular beast was sold I heard someone say: "There's a fool born every minute". His neighbour replied: "Aye, but in this case there were twa fools".

Luckily, Michael and I were not interested in the freshly-calved animals. We were seeking back-end calvers (that is cows which will calve from August onwards), and we were able to procure ten of these at more reasonable rates – though still dear. Local farmers made us pay dearly for the bulling heifers, but we managed to get six. In all, a fair day's buying!

With the cheque handed over and the transport of the cattle arranged with our floater back in Banffshire, we were able to catch the four o'clock ferry back to the mainland. The farther east and north we drove, the drier it became. The service was good and speedy at the hotel in Balinluig where we stopped for a meal, and the long journey back up the A9 was completed in daylight – just. By then we were driving more slowly for we'd already had a seventeen hour day. We still had an hour's drive ahead of us on the slow, twisty road that is the A95.

As we were driving along that lovely little loop road that avoids Grantown there were several fishers standing deep in the River Spey. Just before the bridge, a fisherman came struggling up the bank towards the road carrying a beautiful salmon in his arms. I am no fisherman but I reckoned that shining fish must have been all of twelve pounds. Although it was getting dark by this time, we could clearly see the smile for pleasure on the man's face. Michael and I smiled back and that wasn't difficult because maybe we had smiles on our faces already.

And why? Because we'd had a successful day and because we both felt, inside ourselves, that: "A good day's work is better than a good day's fishing".

A right dressing-down

I can never see lilac but I think of a lass.

Walking through a lovely garden the other day, I came upon a young lilac tree with really pale flowers. The delicate petals were exactly the shade of lilac that I first remember.

It was my second spring at primary school and I was in the higher infant class. I hadn't liked the first two infant teachers and they hadn't liked me.

Ever since I can remember, I have had an aversion to yapping dogs and yapping women. The first two infant mistresses didn't speak – they barked. And they used the ruler on the back of my fingers far too often! My third teacher was very different, though. She spoke softly, and she quickly gained my confidence and co-operation. I suppose it was because I trusted her that a certain incident rankled so much, and has rankled over the years.

My class work must have been quite good because I was promoted to the back row of desks farthest from the teacher's high desk. My companion at the double desk was a quiet lass called Jane and we certainly didn't chatter – well, not much.

The winter had been long and frosty and spring was late in coming. I was still in heavy jerseys, thick socks and boots. The girls wore dark gym tunics and thick stockings well into April.

Then, one Friday, the sun shone from early morning and the classroom became really hot. We country bairns ate our dinner pieces at school, but Jane lived quite near and went home every dinnertime. This hot April day her mother took pity on her, uncomfortable in the heavy clothes, and allowed her to change into a lighter dress for the afternoon.

When the bell rang we all filed into our seats and there, sitting beside me, was this bonnie wee lass in a light summer dress of the palest lilac. I had three sisters who all bossed me, so I wasn't particularly fond of girls. But I had the courtesy to mention to Jane that she was wearing a very pretty dress.

"Yes" she said, "and I've got knickers to match". Without hesitation she lifted her dress to show me. "And I've got a pocket in the leg with a hanky the same colour". Again, she proceeded to show me. I seem to recall that Jane had some difficulty extricating the hanky from the small pocket, so probably the whole process took a minute or two.

Just at that moment, the teacher looked up from her desk and saw us. Well! She went absolutely berserk. Hauling the two of us from our desk by the hair of our heads, she dragged us to the front of the class. The headmistress was summoned and the incident explained to her, doubtless with embellishments.

The entire infant department was hastily mustered to the school hall and Jane and I were paraded in front of the one hundred or so infants. Every misdemeanour, real or imaged, that I had been guilty of in my first year at school was trotted out by the two yapping females while we two "delinquents" stood in holy terror – though completely innocent of any crime. In those days, all female teachers were maiden ladies. Those who married had to resign their posts prior to marriage. A married woman would never return to teaching unless widowed.

So, there stood we two wee mites up on that big stage, being harangued by these three prudes. I'd think it was highly unlikely that anybody had ever been invited to see the colour of their knickers. Had we been sixteen their narrow-mindedness might have been justified; but we were six, for heaven's sake. Such atrocious behaviour as ours had never been known in the infant department, and a pupil was despatched to the primary section to fetch the hardest strap in the school.

When the infant mistress tried to give Jane one stroke on each hand, I sprang forward, wrenched the belt from her hand and threw it right to the back of the hall. That did it! Two teachers grabbed me and forced me to take six whacks on each hand and three across the buttocks. I still can remember how painful it was riding home on the pillion seat of my big sister's bike, but I never breathed a word of the feelings of injustice that boiled inside me.

Although the pendulum has now swung too far the other way and there isn't enough respect shown to teachers at the present time, nevertheless teachers had too much power when I was little. They had the authority to bully and harass and – even worse – the power to discriminate between pupils according to the parents' profession or job. I always felt that many teachers had little time for ferm loons. They reckoned we would just go back to the land, anyway, and I was particularly sorry for cotter bairns.

Of course, it wasn't fashionable to like teachers. The biggest insult your schoolpals could throw at you was to call you the teacher's pet. It wasn't until I was older, much older, that I started to like teachers. In the days before young farmers' clubs took on a matchmaking role, many a farmer's son would depend on the education authority or the district nursing association to bring a suitable lass into the district.

Rural schools had a steady turnover of young women arriving straight from college and teaching just long enough to get their parchment. Then they would swop the drudgery of the classroom for the drudgery of a ferm toun life.

I can clearly remember hurrying home on the first school day after the summer holidays and announcing at the tea table: "We have another teacher in our class and she is spleet new this time". Moreover, this teacher had a spleet new approach to teaching. She could lead, she didn't have to drive.

And I feel sure she would have recognised the innocence of my interest in Jane's lilac dress and underwear.

Effie, the tattie Queen!

That's the tatties finished.

Six drills in the garden are my sole involvement with tatties nowadays, but I never seem to get them finished any earlier than when we grew them in quantity on the farm. Like so much else in farming today, growing potatoes has become the job of a few specialised producers. These men aim for a yield of twenty tons per acre, which is twice what we expected.

Gone, too, are the days when the farm squad would plant a few acres by hand. Usually the foreman horseman was the only person entrusted with the drilling. The rest of the farm squad drove loads of dung straight from the cattle court and forked the muck into the bottom of the drill.

Using his foot as a measure, each man spaced the small seed potatoes a foot apart along the entire length of the field. Then, with great skill, the horseman split the adjoining ridge and covered the tubers. The resultant crop was uncovered by a spinner digger and gathered by a squad of men, women and children, so the presence of stones in the soil was of no importance.

In stark contrast, it is vital that no stones interfere with the complicated potato harvesters. To ensure the smooth operation of these machines, the soil is carefully sifted by a de-stoner which deposits all the stones below working depth in every third drill. Those farmers who have been pressing on with planting potatoes in nearly ideal conditions over the past two weeks are really performing an act of faith. They must be hoping desperately that this year's tattie yield will be much less than it was last year. Any repeat of the 1992 potato glut will ruin many a grower.

Nationally, the over-supply has been so great that many Scottish growers, remote as they are from the main centres of consumption, got no potatoes sold. It is sad to see farms where hundreds of boxes sit full of beautiful potatoes, all growing sprouts, and to realise there's no prospect of a buyer coming along at this late stage in the season.

By June, most modern housewives have gone over to buying early potatoes imported from Egypt or Cyprus. When I was young the last of the main crop was still being used until at least mid-July. Golden Wonders were excellent keepers, and we stored them in a dark shed under sacks which were kept damp.

For many years we had a variety called Edzell Blues. This was also an excellent keeper – even though officially classed as a second early. I seem to recall that it had deep eyes. That would make it unsuitable for today's market.

Rounded potatoes with few, if any, indentations are the consumers' preference. Appearance is now more important than eating quality and varieties like Cara, Estima and Maris Piper are the housewife's choice. These varieities stay whole even if over-boiled, whereas old favourites such as Kerrs Pink are apt to "go through the bree".

I saw in a recent market report that less than forty per cent of the total potato crop in Britain is destined for use as boiling potatoes. The tattie-crisp trade and the instant mashed potato market now take the majority. This is followed closely, of course, by the wonderfully constant demand from the chip-shop trade. Despite many changes in our eating habits, the humble chip shop has remained amazingly popular. I had often heard of chip butties, but I must admit I got a bit of a shock the first time I saw children actually eating sandwiches with just a few limp white potato chips in the centre.

Before tattie crisps were as universal as they are now we used to have a local chip shop which made potato fritters. They were really tasty but they didn't seem to catch on because as far as I know no other chipper tried them. I'm no special lover of potatoes myself and my six short drills will last me from July right through until the end of January. Two boiled potatoes for lunch is about my stretch, but I admit to being a sucker for fried tatties – the crisper the better.

Today's potato growers would need somebody like Effie to keep up consumption. Effie was my mother's cook-kitchen maid for several years. The lass was always good natured and cheery, and she loved peeling tatties. A hundredweight sack lasted only four days. Admittedly, we had lots of men in the kitchen for dinner but none of them equalled Effie when it came to eating tatties.

It was maybe coorse of me to count, but one day I couldn't help noticing. There were only three of us at the table. I took a tattie among my broth – Effie took four and then added a further two. The next course was stew, and Effie started with four good-sized tatties on her plate. Another two followed, then she helped herself to a final two by way of mopping up the gravy.

We must all have worked really hard in those days as midday dinner was always a three-course meal. For dessert we had semolina pudding with rhubarb. The tattie dish was still on the table, so Effie stretched out and took a nice meallie potato on to her pudding plate, just for afters.

Then, so help me, as she rose from the table she reached yet again to the dish and disposed of the one remaining potato – "jist te help awa wi' it", as she said. Sixteen tatties in total at one sitting! It was small wonder that she filled the shafts of the peat barrow better than any man I ever saw.

Speaking about barrows – they say that profits winna hide. Last week, my son Michael came home from the builders' merchants with a spleet new black shining barrow. When chaffed about it, he remarked: "Hang the expense! We deserve a treat now and then".

Miss Bossy Boots in a boilersuit . . .

I can easily feed the calfies.

It is feeding the cats that presents the difficulty. The cats are fussy and so is the boss. My three-year-old grandaughter dishes out the orders, then waits to see that I obey them. Valerie is really not overfond of the calves.

They can be a bit rough with someone so small when jostling to get their noses in the milk buckets. But the cats, all nine of them, do precisely as she orders. Four adult cats have to get their milk outside the small calfhouse. The milk is poured into an old tin drum at an angle to allow all the pussies access at the same time. The next four beauties – last year's crop of kittens – have to be fed in the secure environment of the calf-handling crate where they won't be disturbed.

Then there is Mandy, the mother, the grandmother and possibly the great-gradnmother of the whole brood. She needs special attention when Valerie is around, and is privileged to have a small dish of her very own.

I never grudge the cats an ample supply from the milk setaside for calf-feeding. It's just that the palaver from little Miss Bossy Boots takes up so much time. But then, what else are grandpas for? Valerie insists that all the utensils are meticulously clean before the milk is poured. Grandpa receives fresh instructions each time, as if he couldn't remember from one day to the next. And I daren't hurry over the calf-feeding and use up all the milk because her cats may need a second helping.

Her two elder sisters had a brief spell of coming to the calf-feeding but now; at the big ages of six and eight, they have moved on to higher endeavours. Their after-school time is taken up with Brownies, swimming and Highland dancing. To date, Valerie shows no interest in such ladylike pursuits. As soon as lunchtime is past, she dons her boilersuit and wellies. From then until the work stops for tea around six, she dots on behind her father or grandfather.

Bad weather causes her no concern, and only on frosty days will she deign to wear gloves. With an ample supply on hand-me-down anoraks from her older sisters, Valerie just exchanges one set of soaked clothes for a fresh lot and keeps going. She can be as girny as anything indoors, but the sour face disappears immediately she gets outside. No sooner is she out of the farmhouse door than the ordering starts. "Andy there is a big cow wandering about. You'll have to catch her". And she can usually tell Andy, our dairyman, where the cow was last seen and in which direction she was headed. Or: "Andy, there's too much dubs. You'll have to carry me".

Andy is tall, so from her exalted place high on his shoulders Valerie can issue her orders with ever greater authority. When my own daughter, Maureen, was about the same age back in the 1950s, clothes rationing was still in force. Her mother made her a sirensuit complete with hood to the design made famous by Sir Winston Churchill.

Whenever he was inspecting bomb damage and helping raise morale among the survivors of the blitz, Winston would wear this all-in-one garment – not smart, but immensely practical. Every afternoon Maureen would don her cosy blue suit and

set off over the fields to meet me. You could set your watch to the time that the tiny figure would appear between the large gate posts at the entrance to the farm steading. Then she would toddle the half mile or so to where I was working. Sometimes she would trip on a divot but she always picked herself up and kept coming.

Today, though, Valerie is the proud owner of two boilersuits in the famous tractor and machinery colours – red with a black badge for Massey Ferguson, and green with a yellow badge for John Deere. When she appeared in the Massey Ferguson store in Elgin wearing the wrong boilersuit she got a good ticking off from the storeman. The wee soul was taken aback for a moment before she saw the twinkle in his eye. Then, with a broad smile, she promised to wear his boilersuit when she came back next time.

The other day it was my turn to give her a shoulder carry on our way to the byre. When she noticed Andy some way behind us, she shoulted: "Hurry up, you old stinky bum". I got such a shock I nearly dropped her. I proceeded to give her a good telling-off for using such words. "You must never, ever call anybody an old stink bum", I said. I could see the wee lass thinking for a moment or two.

"Well, hurry up you big stinky bum", she replied, as Andy and I struggled to keep our faces straight. Obviously, I had got my word emphasis misplaced. The tentacles of our education system have enmeshed even our three-year-olds and Valerie has had a couple of terms at playschool.

The other week I had need of a tradesman to do several finnicky jobs at my house. After much phoning around, one arrived. Noticing a photograph of the bairns on the mantelpiece, he exclaimed: "Oh! Are you Valerie's grandad? My wee lad goes to the same playgroup". I thought: "Fame at last!". Anyway, the jobbies were well and quickly done. It just goes to show it isn't what you know but who you know that matters. It seems there is nothing stronger than the old school-tie network – even if in this instance the shared Alma Mater was none other than Portessie Playschool.

Life isn't all one-sided with Valerie. She is a willing wee lass, and since she is swacker than I am she does a lot of fetching and carrying for me. It is highly amusing to see her handling milk drums and feed pails about as big as herself. She will tyave and pech at a job rather than admit it is too hard for her.

If only, as adults, we could retain some measure of a child's pleasure, energy and enthusiasm for even the most mundane tasks, life would indeed remain a great adventure.

Green, green grass of home

The grass is always greener on the other side of the fence, but nae this time. At least, nae for me.

I have been out to look and I've noticed that for once the grass at home is as green as anywhere else. In most years we hope to start cutting grass for silage in the first week of June. Accordingly, I arranged to take a break in the last week of May.

I have a sister who has lived for many years in the middle of England. For her, the North of Scotland ended at Kyle of Lochalsh – as indeed it does for most tourists. I have been trying to persuade her to spare me a week in which I would show her parts that most other tourists do not reach.

The weather is often at its best in the last week in May. It is usually dry and the midgie menace hasn't got going. So we fixed it for last week and duly set off, only this year our silage grass was ready at the same time – the earliest ever for our farm.

It had been my intention to travel up the East Coast to John O'Groats, along the top coast then down the western seaboard. But after being perished by persistent haar for a couple of hours as we viewed the battlements at Fort George, we changed our itinerary and headed inland and west to the brilliant sunshine. About ten miles west of Strathpeffer, we said goodbye to grassy fields and quickly learned what it is like to farm in the Highlands.

The mosses, heathers and natural grasses haven't started to grow yet and the sheep with small, small lambs at foot have to search hard among the humps and hillocks for a subsistence ration. Grass doesn't grow well there until the turn of the day. There were signs that supplementary feeding from hay racks has stopped only within the last few days. It's a pity that both sheep and crofters can't live on beautiful scenery, for that is a commodity present in abundance.

The hard, bare hills and rocky outcrops provide an inhospitable environment for a ewe to rear a lamb, but it nevertheless saddened me to see a sizeable number of ewes going along without offspring.

On a widely-scattered hirsel it is obvious that many ewes never meet up with a tup in the tupping season. As a consequence, lambing percentages can be a mere seventy per cent or even lower. In my eyes, that is bad business for both the sheep owner and for the country.

I wouldn't dare to enter into the argument about whether it is better to lamb ewes on the open hill or in enclosed parks. Throughout the Highlands there are strong advocates of both methods.

Personally, I am utterly convinced that concentration at tupping time would pay dividends. In these days of powerful bulldozers and mechanical diggers there are hillside areas that could be cleared, seeded and fertilised. I have seen it done in the Egyptian desert on equally difficult terrain.

Many land reclamation schemes have been too ambitious, aiming to turn the hillsides into arable land. The creation of reasonable sheep pasture is all I would seek. We who farm the land of the North-east are lucky that our forefathers were such hardworking people, clearing and digging our hillsides. Some of the land they tackled must have had little potential in the early years, but perseverance has brought it to its present high state of production.

Since the demand for small Scottish hill lambs grows stronger every year from discerning buyers in Italy and Spain, it would pay us as a nation to produce more of them. But what is the point in preaching? Most politicians don't know a tup from a toadstool and our nation sinks ever deeper into debt. I know I would not like to be the next Chancellor of the Exchequer when he has to go cap in hand to the IMF.

The sun setting over Loch Shieldaig is a sight that would clear the most furrowed brow. Next morning I thoroughly enjoyed the thrill of descending the steep mountain road from Shieldaig to Kishorn. My sister, however, was not over-impressed. She had tackled worse in Majorca. An afternoon spent among the wonders of Inverewe gardens gladdened her heart, though; and another bonny sunset over Little Loch Broom had her captivated.

Most communities of any size now boast well-appointed museums and Ullapool proved no exception. The troubled and often sad history of the West Highlands makes a fascinating study. Looking at the old photographs, the artefacts and, occasionally, a video presentation fairly runs away with your time.

Then on we went up the hill out of Wester Ross and into Sutherland – into the country that I learned to love when I was the Conservative candidate in 1965/66. The friendliness of its people is unsurpassed anywhere in Scotland. My own special favourite place is the Stoer peninsula. It is largely untouched by tourism, most holidaymakers hurrying past the end of it. The single-track roads are so narrow that no buses can penetrate. I hope things stay that way.

Eventually, we came across a fold of pure Highland cattle and stopped to admire them. As well as the usual reds there were brindles, blacks and one cream beauty. Their calves were small and still furry-faced so we took a few snapshorts,

"An afternoon spent among the wonders of Inverewe gardens gladdened her heart, though . . ."
Picture courtesy of the National Trust for Scotland

although neither my sister nor I are any great shakes with a camera. Two of the cows were standing in the middle of the road but we were in no hurry to move them. Then along came a driver in a camper van. He jumped out, shooed the cows off the road and hastily jumped back behind the wheel, shouting as he passed us: "There is no need to be frightened of them". So saying, he smugly drove on.

The sea lochs, the fresh-water lochs and the deserted beaches of white sand all looked inviting in the exceptionally clear light that is a special feature of the Stoer/Clachtoll/Clachnessie area. Time just flew by.

We could well have lingered longer in the West, for the moment we turned the top corner past Cape Wrath and down into Durness, the warm sun left us. But the welcome at the first bed and breakfast we called at could not have been warmer. "You are Hamish Watt or I'm a Dutchman", said genial host and crofter Mr Campbell.

He and I commiserated with each other about the unnecessary complication of the IACS forms. I also sympathised with him on the vexed subject of transport charges. I get about £1 for a small bale of hay, but by the time it reaches Durness it costs £2 or more.

The highlight of our stay had to be the beautiful soda scones baked fresh each morning for breakfast by Mrs Campbell. Who needs butteries?

A quick phonecall back to base assured me that the silage-making was progressing well without me. I didn't know whether to be pleased or miffed that I wasn't being missed. But Caithness and Orkney beckoned.

Search ends with oat cuisine

For a long time now I have been looking for a place that Kelloggs haven't reached. At Durness I found it. The creamy porridge Mrs Campbell makes is an art form that Mr Kellogg hasn't been able to copy.

Rumour has it that the oatmeal came from Portsoy. Anyway, the plateful of porridge and the memorable soda scones provided my sister and I with a breakfast that sustained us throughout a day of motoring along the sea lochs of North-west Scotland.

We had to stop briefly at Tongue so that I could post back to Durness the bedroom key that was still in my pocket. I was grateful to the postmistress for her helping in parcelling and labelling. You'd think I would learn!

No trip to that part of the world would be complete without visiting the excellent museum in the converted church at Bettyhill. We also took time to look around the pre-Clearances village nearby. I forget the name, but the ambience and general features of the place will long remain a vivid memory.

Life must have been very harsh in such primitive conditions. Undoubtedly, changes were necessary; but there was no excuse for the tactics employed by the Duchess of Sutherland and her agent, Patrick Sellar.

With a more enlightened policy of education, land and livestock improvement and farm amalgamations, the land-owning gentry could have acquired increased income without inflicting the suffering and misery which will forever be associated with the Clearances. Strathalladale and Strathnaver were subjected to similar treatment, but I shall keep them for another shudder, as we look back on "man's inhumanity to man".

There is now hardly a loch that doesn't have its quota of salmon cages. It is really heartening to see an industry that helps to keep the menfolk employed in these remote areas. It is also easy to see how young men from such a background, with their wide knowledge of both land and sea, are so welcomed by the oil industry.

There is now a whole generation of young men who have served an excellent apprenticeship along the coast at Dounreay as welders, fitters, engineers, electricians and so forth. Their technical skills are in great demand on oilrigs in the North Sea and throughout the world. Moreover, having been reared on the cold North Coast they have an extra attribute. They have the ability to survive and get on with the job in constant wind, rain and cold – something their city-reared counterparts lack.

I first toured the Dounreay complex in 1965. I remember being very impressed at the time, and I was impressed yet again last week by the unbelievably strict measures everybody takes to ensure plant safety. When you come down out of the Sutherland hills the first sight of the huge atomic sphere on the far coast is very striking. But alas, the farmer in me soon takes over.

I became fascinated by the vast difference in the farming scene. The open moorland gives way to enclosed fields. There are well maintained dry stone dykes and whole fields that are "fenced" by flat Caithness slate slabs, carefully set up to break the wind.

However, the greatest contrast lies in the sheer size of the cattle and the sheep. The big, strong-framed North Country Cheviot ewes must be twice as heavy as their counterparts on the Sutherland hills.

The cattle and sheep were lying well content in lush green grass, with food a-plenty in their bellies. A far cry from the scrape-hard existence endured by the hill sheep just a few miles back.

Although born and reared in the uplands, I have always been very fond of the sea, and in the entire journey from Durness to John O'Groats you rarely lose sight of the Pentland Firth.

Our next two-night stop was at a comfortable new bungalow overlooking the pier at Huna, close by John O'Groats. Even in the late-night dim I couldn't put down my binoculars for watching the constant passage of boats round Dunnet Head. Next morning, the Pentland Firth was like a mill pond for our forty-five minute crossing from John O'Groats to Burwick. Our tour bus was waiting at the far end of the pier.

The driver/courier for the next eight hours was a breezy young lad who told his captive audience tales nearly as tall as Charlie Allan's. Although not an Orcadian by birth, he obviously loves his adoptive islands. Maybe the high winds are a beneficial factor, but for whatever reason the farms seemed incredibly tidy, with no plastic fertiliser bags stuck on the fences.

I had always known that Orkney cattle and sheep were good, but I'd forgotten just how good. The Orkney stock we see at Thainstone market often look jaded after their long journey. On their home ground they look tremendous.

There are still lots of Aberdeen-Angus cows around. If that once-dominant breed is to make the comeback our supermarket meat buyers are predicting, then Orkney is the place that will benefit most.

I saw many excellent Charolais and Simmental bulls running with the big-bodied black cows. Sadly, the two black Angus bulls that I did notice were no credit to the breed. Like nearly every Canadian-bred Angus, these were too long in the leg and totally devoid of flesh on the hips.

I was reminded of the AA cattle field day at a farm which must be nameless. After the imported animals had been duly paraded, Charlie McCombie, of Auchincrieve, Rothiemay, was heard to remark: "Right. We have seen the front ends. When are you going to import the back ends?" That incident happened some years ago, but the back ends have not yet appeared.

This holiday was really my sister's. We gave Kirkwall, Stromness, Scapa Flow and Skara Brae a thorough lookover. We explored every standing stone and burial ground in the vicinity.

She will now be able to tell her English friends that here in the North we have some stone circles that are taller than Stonehenge and some that are a thousand years older than Stonehenge. And we have a lot more of them, forbye.

Our enjoyable holiday would have been even more enjoyable had the lovely weather of the West accompanied us to Caithness and Orkney. Despite some memorable whisky toddies from Stromness to Dornoch, I caught a cold. And it served me right.

Ne'er cast a cloot till May be oot. Well, I did and I paid the price. I needed two days in bed to throw it off, and by that time the green grass at home was all in the silage pit in record time. And all accomplished without any help from me.

Minding our language

"Never follow the herd", my father used to say; and I try wherever possible to avoid using the themes of other journalists and broadcasters.

Still, I would be downright churlish if I failed to acknowledge the excellence of the Grampian Television programme, *Troubled Fields*. Frieda Morrison has done an outstanding job in portraying farming life in the North-east. I know Charlie Allan paid his tribute last week, and for this once I am broadly in agreement with his sentiments. But I have aye my reservations about Charlie.

I mean to say, who in their right senses would go looking for arnuts on a spring day? Surely every countryman knows that October is the time when the arnuts – or corms – are at their fullest and freshest.

Having got that bee out of my bonnet, *Troubled Fields* troubled me. The current problems facing many of our small and middle-sized farms were well highlighted. I twas truly sad to see the Jaffreys, father and son, deciding to give up the unequal struggle. No one can blame the young lad for opting for the safety of a guaranteed pay packet rather than continuing to seek his livelihood in the high-risk farming industry.

We have to remember, though, that we have had good years in farming as well as bad; and right now it certainly looks as if this year will be a good one for those of us who stuck to livestock. In the past, too many farmers listened to the experts who advocated going down the road of monoculture. "Get rid of the livestock and concentrate on grain-growing" they said.

Well, I did improve my grain growing, but at the same time I increased the stock we carried. The extra straw was converted into valuable feed by having the bales wrapped and injected with ammonia. Both sheep and cattle, and even young calves, are really fond of the smelly stuff and they thrive well on it. The last of the overwintered stirks have now been sold; and all of them have left a better margin of profit than ever before.

It is easy to understand how many farmers did follow the herd, however. College advisers and bankers often sing each others' tunes, and vulnerable folk act on their advice and instructions.

I will admit there have been times when I wondered if I was just being bloody-minded – especially when we were reeling under Maggie Thatcher and her money lenders' Government. None of our farming enterprises could for long withstand interest rates of twenty per cent or more. Yet, that is what the bank was charging us for nearly three years.

Of course, it was tempting to sell off the stock, lessen the overdraft and at the same time cut the wages bill, but I'm glad I resisted. Sadly, the Jaffreys and many hundreds like them had to go down that road.

Now, "that" road has led to "down the road". Added to the financial burden are the problems caused by the Common Agricultural Policy with its complicated programmes of set-aside. Maximum production from our land is no longer required and this goes against the grain with most hardworking North-east farmers.

Over the past four years those farmers who could no longer survive financially, together with those who chose to give up the unequal struggle, put their farms up for sale. Luckily, there were buyers for most of them.

Exactly the same set of circumstances applied back in the 1920s and through most of the 30s. As a young lad, I can remember empty, derelict farms scattered along whole stretches of the Glen of Foudland. It wasn't until the war years that the land was farmed again. At that time there were no buyers for the farms which came on the market. This time, we've seen English people sell their own farms in the South and buy four times the acreage up here.

We should really be grateful to the English among us, not resentful. Yet, I couldn't help feeling, as I watched *Troubled Fields*, that there was a tendency for the English buyers to be cast as the villains of the piece. Time alone will tell whether the majority of newcomers manage to prosper in the colder climate and less fertile soil. I, for one, wish them well. After all, I have uncles and cousins who prospered after taking the bold step of moving to England to farm. If the reverse works, that is all right by me.

I cannot agree with the other theme of Frieda's programme in which she suggested that our culutre may be at risk because of the arrival of the "sooth moothers" (if I can borrow an Orkney and Shetland phrase to describe the English buyers). The use of the Doric was declining long before they came – although I am heartened to hear children still using their native tongue among themselves. I am sure many of the new arrivals must wonder what their bairns are saying when they come home from school with the language of the playground.

The long-term survival of Doric will only be assured, however, if it is fostered in our schools, just as Gaelic now is in Highland schools. The very recent move to encourage Doric in the classroom, with the appointment of an adviser in Doric teaching, is a big change from my young day when you earned six skelps of the tag for using Doric words.

The really important thing is to keep our children bi-lingual. They ought to be allowed to speak the Doric at home, while at the same time being encouraged to become fluent in English against the day when they have to mix in the big wide world. The last thing we want is to foster North-east nationalism where the password would be: "Fit like?"

Among our children there is an in-built inclination to use the Doric, and this makes me optimistic about its survival. I remember when my daughter Maureen was five and just starting to read. I can hear her yet as she sat in the big rocking chair, trying to make sense of the words. "T-O-P, top" she said. "T-A-P, tap", and finally, "T-I-P, cowp", she announced.

Congratualations on giving us an excellent programme, Frieda. But next time, listen to the children.

Pipes of peace . . .

A customer called at the farm last week.

He was looking for a Friesian cow to rear two pedigree bull calves. We showed him three which we thought would fill the bill and supplied him with the particulars of each one. Next we told him the prices we were expecting.

On our farm customers are the most important people around and we like to encourage them wherever possible. We could have the most marvellous cattle ever but unless we have customers to buy them we couldn't survive. Maybe we made a mistake offering the farmer too wide a choice or maybe the prices asked gave him a fleg.

He said never a word, just took from his pocket the shortest pipe I have ever seen. Off came the lid and with two matches he lit a fire right under his nose. He puffed and puffed until his head was in a cloud of tobacco reek. Then ever so slowly he took the pipe from his mouth, spat a couple of times, and proclaimed: "Dammit boys, you're some steep".

My three grand-daughters, who had been watching the performance were wide-eyed with wonder. They had honestly never seen a man smoking a pipe and it was when they were telling their mother of this strange carry-on afterwards that I realised just how few folk smoke pipes nowadays. Although pipe smokers are less likely to contract cancer than are cigarette smokers, somehow it seems that it is the pipe smokers who have heeded the health warnings.

At the time when I smoked there were shops in our high streets which prospered selling smoking materials only. Long after I had abandoned the habit and conquered the craving, I still loved to pass the open door of a good tobacconist. The aroma of the fine tobaccos went round my heart in the same way as peat reek still does. I never regarded myself as a serious pipe smoker because I also smoked cigarettes and two ounces of an expensive blend, which I came across in South Africa near the end of the war, lasted me more than a week.

But when I was nineteen and knew it all, a pipe clenched between the teeth added a touch of maturity, or so I thought at the time. I later found that most British blends were too strong for me. Even St Bruno was too heavy and I made do with Erinmore mild. Most men on our farms smoked far stronger tobaccos such as Condor Plug, Tam O'Shanter, or the horseman's favourite, Bogie Roll.

In 1954, when I started farming on my own account, I had a grieve of the old school. Ed was an excellent manager of men and was never seen idle himself. Every yoking time he had three filled pipes in his pockets so he never had to spend time on a refill. All his pipes were the same – medium short Steenhives – that is Stonehavens. These came in three lengths, short, medium short and medium. I never heard of long Steenhives but there may have been such.

There was a method in the grieve's use of only one kind of pipe. Pipes often got broken at work and if some of Ed's broke the pieces were interchangeable. He never found himself in the position of other men I knew who would break or lose their pipe and have to go for the rest of the day without a smoke. Everybody else on the farm then had to thole their bad temper.

When I was very young my aunties had an old auntie they never spoke about in polite company. They were "black affronted" by her because the old dear smoked Bogie Roll in a clay pipe. In those pre-war days of the 30s only tinker wifies and such smoked pipes so having this old bedridden smoker in one's house was "an unco come doon"! She kept her clay cutty up the chimney and could spit from her bed to the fireplace. And, what was worse, she lived to be 101.

But it is to John Pirie, who used to farm at Bogmoon in Cairnie, that I am indebted for the best smoking stories. He was telling me that his father gave him an old pipe when he was only ten and would hand him a small piece of twist each morning. John kept his pipe in a hole in the school dyke at Alehousehillock School in Cairnie. He would ask to leave the room for a call of nature and have a sly smoke. That made him sick so he would then be sent home. A little later his pal would try the same caper with the same pipe. If the ploy worked, the two would truant for the rest of the day. "But dominies werna feel", said John and the schoolmaster went searching for the offending pipe and duly found it.

None of the pupils would admit to ownership and John's precious possession was thrown in the back of the classroom fire. He remembers clearly the replacement pipe that he had to boil to reduce its pungency and then break in gently to avoid burning the bowl. Bogie Roll proved too strong for the young lad and he had to settle for Erinmore, which he smokes to this day. He is now 79 and hale and hearty.

At the Boghead shop where John bought his tobacco the twist was not weighed, but was measured against marks on the grocery counter and then cut by a guillotine. John remembers having to fetch home tobacco for an old uncle and aunt. His aunt would unroll the tobacco, fold it over, and with a quick twist she would divide it equally. She then handed one half to her husband and stuffed her share into the cavernous front pocket of her pinnie.

The old couple sat at a big open fire puffing their clay cutties contentedly. Perfect harmony reigned in that house where the uncle lived to be 100 and the auntie to 103.

There seems to be no doubt that smoking a pipe has a soothing effect. My customer of last week puffed away and spat away. He upped his offer and I cut the asking price. We haggled in great good humour and finally agreed on a figure. But I sure am glad that nowadays we no longer spit on our palms before shaking hands on a deal . . .

A Stinging tale . . .

What a fleg I got.

I was driving on a side road near Clochan and just as I passed a gap in the hedge my windscreen went black.

In the past, I have experienced the shock of driving blind when a windscreen shattered but this was different.

The windscreen and the windows on the passengers' side were completely blacked out. My car had been hit by a swarm of bees. By good luck, both windows were fully closed; and fortunately there was no other traffic on the road, for I'm sure I must have swerved violently.

I'm terrified of bees and for good reason, so I switched on my wipers, washers and all. As soon as I could see out reasonably well, I put on speed and kept going until the slipstream had blown all the insects away. Then I stopped and just sat there, shaking and sweating.

In a way I was sorry to have scattered the swarm, but I was immensely relieved that I hadn't been stung. If either of the side windows had been open I doubt if I would have been writing this story.

I have a love-hate relationship with bees. I like them but their stings don't like me. Most of my uncles kept lots of bees and were real enthusiasts. One, Jim Allan, of Stoneytown Farm in Mulben, regularly kept fifty to sixty hives as well as straw skeps which he used for trapping stray swarms before decanting them into a permanent hive.

Quite often if a swarm was small he would remove the queen bee and merge the swarm with another to form a stock strong enough to withstand the cold of their first winter.

A fellow bee enthusiast and willing helper was the local schoolmaster Mr Hector Gunn. The two of them, Mr Gunn and my uncle, could regularly be seen moving the hives away in the early summer and back near to the farm in the late autumn. They used a wee sheltie and a flat-bottomed spring cart with maybe six hives aboard.

Bees are kittle cattle to handle at any time and the six hives made a fikey load. On one occasion, some of the bees escaped and stung the pony. The poor beast went berserk and they had no option but unharness it from the float or the load would have been tipped.

With the pony rapidly heading for home, the resourceful schoolmaster got between the shafts and pulled the cart and load the two mile to the farm while Jim Allan pushed from behind.

I was delighted to be able to confirm the tale with Mr Gunn recently. Although well over eighty, he is hale and hearty and still looks strong enough to get between the shafts. He thought my uncle did a marvellous job unhitching the pony when it was plunging so violently.

I do not know if the headmaster augmented his salary with his hives but Jim Allan always declared that his bees paid his farm rent and carried the farm through the depression years. My bee stock had grown from one gift hive up to nine strong stock in 1965, and I genuinely liked working with the bees, feeding them with blocks of candy sugar in the winter and checking that mice did not get into the hives.

Mice apparently are totally immune to bee stings – either that or the bees are too dozy all winter to fight back. Anyway, I have seen a strong stock of many thousands reduced to less than a hundred survivors by just one mouse. Only the wings get left uneaten.

In hot July days, newly-hatched queen bees gather some worker bees around them and leave the parent hive. The "top", or first, swarm can consist of half of the total bees in the hive. As a lad, one summer job that I hated was being ordered to follow a swarm to see where it landed. The hotter the day the farther the swarm flew and it was difficult to keep it in sight. If I lost it, I could count on getting a good telling-off.

Should the swarm land in a neighbour's farmyard, he would claim it unless it had obviously been followed from the original farm. Otherwise, it was a case of finder's keepers. When the swarm landed on a fence post or the branch of a tree a ladder, a white sheet, and a straw skep sprinkled with honey were used to recapture the escapees in the cool of the evening.

1965 was a good year for honey production. My catastrophe happened the day I was removing a good crop of clover honey and replacing the laden boxes with new sections, ready for the heather honey harvest. My smoking bellows went out and I hurried to the house for more corrugated cardboard to get it going again. While there, the phone rang and I spent ten minutes newsing to a neighbour.

When I eventually returned to the hives the bees were thoroughly worked up and flew straight at me. Although I was wearing gloves, hat and veil correctly, the sheer weight of their numbers pressed the veil against my throat and neck. Within seconds, I got about forty stings. I immediately felt queer and made for the house to phone the doctor, but by the time I had gone the fifty yards or so my legs were useless and I fell into the back porch.

My wife phoned the doctor at once, then helped me upstairs to bed. I couldn't use my hands, then I couldn't see, then my voice faded and I began to have difficulty in breathing. I started slipping in and out of consciousness and I knew I was dying when I heard the doctor rush into the room.

"Boil a kettle", he shouted, then took one look at me and said: "No! Never mind! There isn't time". With that he slammed a huge anti-histamine injection into my arm. Then he pulled me into a sitting position and forced about three pints of very salty water through my clenched teeth. That made me violently sick and as soon as I started to throw up I came back from the dark tunnel and I knew I was going to live.

The doctor stayed with me until midnight then he called again at noon next day. "Right, you can resume normal duties" said Dr Simmers. "We can laugh about it now, but if I hadn't been sitting at the other end of the phone and if I hadn't been in the habit of driving a fast car you'd have been a gonner last night".

I related the near tragedy to my mother some days later. "Oh aye, I could have told you that you were allergic to bee stings", she said casually. "We nearly lost you when you were four. You went rigid after being stung in the throat. That time, we brought you round by plunging you in hot and cold baths, time about, but it was a near thing".

It's great how you can go off folk – and bees.

White knight and missing coo . . .

It was like a scene from *Fawlty Towers*. Or, to be more accurate, like a sketch from *Scotland the What?*

You see, I'm not very well acquaint with the Methlick area and I had to ask for directions to Charlie Allan's farm.

As I came in the low road from Fyvie, a car drew up alongside two young housewives who were having a chat at their garden gates. The car driver – a well-built bloke in a blue boiler suit and a black beard – joined them. "Just the folk I need to tell me the way" I thought. I stopped my car and got out.

The face above the beard grinned broadly when the man recognised me, and the eyes twinkled. "Along to the T-junction, turn left, then go right up the hill to the road second on the left – and stop telling lees aboot him".. All this before I could utter a word!

It was exactly the answer I wanted, of course, only I never yet got the chance to put the question. All four of us were laughing as I said my thanks and got back into the car. It could only happen in Buchan.

His directions were spot on. I was just ten minutes late for my appointment with the big man. I wanted to pick his brains about a project I have never tackled before.

Little Ardo was looking well. The contractor's silage squad was baling, carting and wrapping a heavy cut of grass from a very steep field. With the exception of some of the grass parks down by the River Ythan, many of Charlie's fields are brae-set and four-wheel tractors must be a godsend in such conditions.

In stark contrast, most of the fields on my own farm are flat as a book and we have little need of extra pulling power in the front wheels of our tractors.

I enjoyed my half-hour tour of the farm and was impressed with how well his crops are looking. As with my own, a lot will depend on the weather we get between now and harvest. Any excess rain will most assuredly flatten the winter barley on both our farms. Then we will be easy prey to every passing pigeon and crow. Both of us have grown a six-rowed variety of winter barley in the belief, or rather the hope, that birds find it more difficult to attack than the normal two-rowed variety.

Now I know that Charlie is in constant competition with his neighbours as to who gets the highest tonnage per acre from the crops of barley, wheat and oilseed rape. As his crops are mostly sold to merchants, Charlie has weight tickets to back up his claims.

On our farm, virtually all of the barley is retained as feed for our cattle, so we record our yields solely by the number of grain bins filled from a particular field. Finer points such as bushel weight and the nitrogen content of the barley are of no interest to us. Many of the crops I saw on my bus trip to Ingliston were light and open, but fortunately Charlie and I both seem destined to have a really good crop of straw. It is just a pity that Methlick is so far from Buckie because I would give him a bid for his surplus bales.

I'd better not say any more about Charlie's farming in case his white knight in the blue boiler suit accuses me of telling more lees aboot him. Still, although I had only a quick look at his beef cows and their calves, I would nearly swear that I didn't see a "blue grey coo".

The trip round the farm in a diesel car took little more than half-an-hour. In days gone by such a visit, especially the first one, would have occupied a hale forenicht (evening).

During the past winter I met Alex Smith, the elderly farmer from Banff who after his retirement wrote three books about farming life. He told me he'd had great difficulty in getting them published because they are written entirely in the Doric and only he could proof read for accuracy. His publisher was in Ipswich, I think, and hadn't a clue about the meaning of most of the words.

The only book of Alex's that I've had time to read so far is *Ferming As It Was*. It describes in immense detail the day-to-day work on a farm in the 1930s. I think Alex must have recorded everything conscientiously in daily diary reports over the years in order to be able to give such a clear picture after all all this time. We are fortunate to be left with such a definite record. In producing his books Alex undoubtedly had to work as hard as he'd ever done. I was saddened to see from a recent *Press and Journal* that the grim reaper had caught up with him.

Meanwhile, at the other end of the age spectrum little Miss Bossy Boots – who is three and would dearly like to be four – is a gey quiet lass these days. She is in the doghouse for doing what many another little girl has done. She took a big scissors to her own hair. I'd say she made a good job of it for a first attempt, but her mother thinks differently. Her light brown hair with fair tints used to be chin length but now it doesn't reach to the top of her ears.

Anyway, the hairdresser did a passable job of trimming the lot and now I have a sad wee facey with a boy's crop on top following me around. I'm sure her tresses will have grow back almost to their usual length before her birthday three months from now. It's a pity that her shearings couldn't have been used to thicken up her grandfather's "light and open" crop of hair.

I sometimes think my head is like a set-aside park – there's practically nothing growing there.

Lament for black beauty

Oh dear me! I've made a backside of things again.

A couple of weeks ago I stated that the champion Aberdeen-Angus cow at the Highland Show had no Canadian blood in her. Well, I was quite wrong and will readily admit it and do apologise. It was the backside of the cow that misled me. While many Canadian-bred animals lack decent hindquarters, this excellent cow was as good a specimen as any lover of the ancient breed could possibly ask for.

As a one-day only visitor to the show I had no time to study all the animals in detail so I didn't bother to buy a catalogue or I would have read that the beast had been imported from Canada.

If only I had chatted in more serious vein to Charlie McCombie at the A-A judging ring, he might have pointed out to me that in the case of this cow the owner had imported a back-end as well as a fore-end. Anyway, I congratulate the owner of such a magnificent animal and hope that she will pass on to her progeny that elusive backside that used to be the hallmark of the Aberdeen-Angus breed.

The first rap over the knuckles was a good-humoured letter from the master raconteur of the Scottish farming scene, Captain Ben Coutts, from Crieff. Ben was for several years secretary of the Aberdeen-Angus society and as long ago as the 70s he advocated using the best cows in Scotland, whether pedigree or not, to put back size into the breed.

Incidentally, Captain Coutts tells me he has only recently discovered the delights of the *Farm Journal* and is now a regular reader of its columns.

But it is a true saying that "kail at hame is nae kitchie" and both the Angus breeders and the Friesian breeders sought size from Canada, and both lost in the doing of it, that elusive thing called quality.

The next letter, however, was in a very different vein, coming as it did from the current secretary of the Aberdeen-Angus society. He fails to realise that my criticism of today's black bulls is made "more in sorrow than in anger".

I was brought up using black bulls on our dairy cows which produced good quality calves for commercial farmers to rear on for beef production. There would have been no thought of changing breeds if the blacks had continued to breed rangy calves but all of a sudden during the 60s the breed lost size.

But to go farther back to when I was a schoolboy, Angus cattle were the only kind to be seen in our countryside. Certainly, some farmers had Shorthorn bulls but the beef stirks were almost always black.

I well remember hearing that a farmer three miles down the Huntly road had bought a strange red bull with a white face and long horns. It was called a Hereford and quite the first in the district. I was determined to see it at the first opportunity – but it meant cycling uphill all the way. Bikes were slow and heavy and it was common practice for us loons to grab the end of a passing lorry and get pulled along.

Whether the driver had a mirror on his off-side I know not, but we never got a row, even though we were indulging in a somewhat dangerous practice. It was easy to let go when we reached our destination. In retrospect I doubt if the lorries exceeded twenty miles an hour on the flat and a lot less up a brae.

HF Miss Tip Top, the Canadian-bred five-and-a-half-year-old Aberdeen-Angus cow from Mr George Forbes-Leith, Fyvie Estates, which too the breed championship and went on to take the beef interbreed individual title at the Royal Highland Show

Indeed, the coal fired steam wagons only did about fifteen miles an hour. I just remember them as they were rapidly being superseded by petrol-driven lorries by the time I was a competent cyclist.

Anyway one dry Friday afternoon I had got myself a good hitch on to a lorry and decided that I would stay with it all the way until I reached the Hereford bull. My right arm was gye tired but I got there quickly and effortlessly. The bull certainly was big and impressive and his bright ruby red colour was a welcome change from the eternal black of all our cattle at home.

Try as I would, however, I couldn't persuade my father even to go and look at the beast. It was to be thirty years later before he bought his first Hereford bull.

My father hated buying and selling and I was left to get on with it from an early age. In the early 50s I was sent to Elgin to buy a bull at the spring sale. I bought the very last bull in the catalogue and got a "thief's" bargain. For £105 I acquired a Dounseside-bred bull and my father had him for sixteen years.

Dad always declared that bull could count. He would be turned into a field with a batch of heifers and be expected to stay there. Normally twenty-one days are required to ensure that all the heifers have come into season and been mated. But often the old bull would jump the fence and come home to his comfy loosebox after only sixteen days – his task completed. And sure enough nine months later the heifers would calve down within the sixteen days, all producing good, perky calves, little replicas of their sire.

The shape and size of the Angus calf makes for easy delivery and difficult calvings were virtually unknown from Robert MacRobert, as we affectionately called the old lad after his breeder, Lady MacRobert of Douneside at Tarland.

In stark contrast my brother Percy paid 3,000gn in Perth for the last Angus bull he bought four years ago. The beast had Canadian breeding on both sides of his pedigree.

"Well", says Percy, "that bull bred goats, he bred donkeys, he bred things like whippet dogs – but he never bred anything that remotely resembled a decent black calf". So I reckon the Aberdeen-Angus breed has still a lot to do to regain the confidence of those of us who would still prefer to use Angus bulls.

And I am sad to say that some of today's Angus breeders are falling into the same trap as many politicians do: they believe their own propaganda.

Call of the West . . .

The very name Tarbert (Loch Fyne) sends out seductive signals inviting you to come west for a visit.

But the next line of the advert – Tarbert Fair day show and sale of dairy cattle – proved irresistible. So off I set for Argyll in my old Japanese car which has taken a new lease of life since it went sailing through its MOT test.

In late July the hills of Scotland are at their greenest, just before the heather turns purple and the bracken turns yellow, then brown.

I am a great believer in using the night to make the day longer so I travelled down in the early evening via Aviemore and Pitlochry before turning west. The road from Kenmore to Killin, along the north shores of Loch Tay, must rank as one of the most beautiful roads in Scotland.

After the bed-and-breakfast tourists had left the road, the journey was faster than expected. Crianlarich and Ardlui were quickly behind me and I was running down the shores of Loch Lomond at sunset to Tarbet, the gateway to Argyll. Here the mountains crowd in close to the road and I mused of the days when I knew the local laird, Michael Noble, who was also the local Member of Parliament and Tory Secretary of State for Scotland.

Back in the 60s he and I would discuss the merits of the recently introduced sheep subsidy. He was in favour of paying subsidy on the ewe on the hill, whereas I believed, as I still do, that the subsidy should be paid on the finished lamb when it comes to market. Michael Noble readily admitted that on his own estate he

A tranquil scene at Tarbert by the shores of Loch Fyne
Picture courtesy of PA News

achieved only a fifty-four per cent lambing average. As the ewe lambs had to be retained to keep up the ewe numbers, his estate was selling only one lamb for every four ewes which were drawing subsidy.

But I will always be grateful to the Noble family for their pioneering of oyster farming in Argyll. Just before the Oyster Bar closed at 9pm I called in for a memorable meal of six prime oysters served with brown bread and a glass of white wine. That's what I call living! Loch Fyne kept me company on the lefthand side as I motored past Inveraray with its menacing castle and fearsome gaol which could tell many a tale of dark deeds and treachery.

The loch, with its outlet to the sea and its connection with the Clyde, was busy with yachts anchored everywhere. One day, I promise myself, I will join one of these yachts on a trip through the Crinan canal. But right now, with only coos on my mind, I pressed on in the dark to Ardishaig to the guesthouse where I had booked a room.

Often, after a tiring car journey, I "thunder on" long after I've gone to bed, but in the soft air of the West I slept well and rested. Next morning at breakfast I noticed I was the only guest in what must be a six-bedroom establishment. Small wonder there is a veritable forest of For Sale signs on the big houses throughout Perthshire and Argyll.

I breakfasted well on porridge and Loch Fyne kippers. The porridge was fine and kippers were scrumptious. I like breakfasting on kippers in hotels and restaurants for no matter how I try to cook them, the smell of kipper pervades my own house for days.

The weather in the West was the same as we have at home in the North – rain and more rain – and I was thankful that Tarbert Mart could boast a roof, even though there were wet draughts blowing through. You see, the modern mart complex at Inverurie with its creature comforts have spoiled us North-east farmers and we take badly now to the rigours that have to be tholed at other marts.

But the cattle were good and I managed to buy five nice in-calf heifers, although buyers from Cheshire and Shrewsbury had deeper purses than I. As at all other marketing centres, the number of dairy animals for sale is declining. At Tarbert there was a great show of beef animals, but I didn't wait to see them sold.

On impulse, for a change of scenery, I decided to go home by another route. I had just turned on to the Oban road at Lochgilphead when I was thumbed by two very drookit girl hitchhikers. They were standing in a downpour such as only the West of Scotland can lay on and so I broke my usual rule of no lifts. They turned out to be Polish students studying English at Cracow University, who were on their second visit to Scotland, rain and midges notwithstanding. Their command of English was excellent and their cheery conversation made the long stretch of low road shortsome.

That particular piece of Argyll always puts me in mind of the Somerset farmer who took part in an exchange visit with some dairy farmers in Morayshire. He had motored through the Welsh hills, then the Yorkshire moors and on by the moors of Lanarkshire and the A9 to Grantown. Finally, he reached Forres by way of the Dava moor. At the reception that night I asked him how he had enjoyed his journey. "I have never seen so much 'damn all' in my life", was the answer I shall never forget.

It is more than high time that much of the land of Argyll, which at present grows only bracken, should be put to growing some decent conifers. I enjoyed the company of the hitchhikers as far as Oban. After that, for the rest of the journey, I had only the scenery and the unwelcome company of the breakfast kippers.

As usual Fort William was shrouded in mist, but at Fort Augustus the sun was shining. Every lay-by along the entire length of Loch Ness was packed with sightseers. With cameras at the ready they were doubtless hoping to be as lucky as the two lads from Culbokie, who claim to have captured Nessie on film. Whether or not they have succeeded, the youngsters should get the Queen's Award for Export Achievement as they will undoubtedly bring in more badly needed foreign visitors.

Round the corner at Drumnadrochit and I was on the home straight. I was thrilled to see that some fields of winter barley had already been combined – our own can't be long in following. It was great to have visited again the mountains and the lochs of the West, but my favourite part of Scotland is the well-cultivated lowlands along the Moray coast. We don't have a very wide coastal plain but oh, it is kindly land.

I'm sure the heifers will thrive and do well.

Wet, wet, wet shows . . .

I've fairly been pushing the boat out. Four agricultural shows in one year is well beyond my usual.

What with a long day at the Highland Show in June, followed by a day each at Turriff, Black Isle and Keith shows I must have been skiving from the summer's farm work.

People I meet tell of equally wet summers but 1993 ranks among the wettest I can remember. A similar year occurred in the late 50s when I didn't get my hay finished until after harvest, only things weren't so mechanised then and much of the work was done by hand with pitchforks. That year we got no good hay whereas this year the early-baled fields were secured in good order and stacked inside before the rains came.

We should have been finished totally by this time and have only ourselves to blame. A late offer from a neighbour of five acres of good grass could not be refused. Now, for days we have been waiting in vain for twenty-four dry hours in order to turn the bouts of very wet grass.

It is the show organisers that I am really sorry for this year. Throughout the twelve months committees put in a lot of thought and effort to ensure the success of their show. But if it rains on the day much of their work is wasted.

I have paid tribute before now to the dedication of those who take their stock to agricultural shows. Now I have to add my thanks to the vast army of horse-lovers who brave the elements to show their favourite cuddies. Seriously though, the sight of the arena at Turriff Show on the Monday afternoon was quite magnificent, with nearly six hundred ponies of all descriptions parading in front of an appreciative audience.

I loved especially the display of Highland garrons at the Black Isle Show. Those with the deer carrying panniers or harness were particularly impressive. But what stands out most of all is the tremendous parades of Clydesdale horses at all the events this year. It seems a pity that a working role cannot be found on our farms for the big, able, likeable brutes. They would provide a cheap source of motive power if only we weren't all in such a hurry.

Everyone seems to take it for granted that an alternative source of power will be found by the time we have exhausted the world's reserves of oil and gas. Mark you, I for one, wouldn't like to go back to being totally dependent on horsepower. when I did work with horses and shelts, cuts were commonplace from both horseshoes and shoenails. Every three years I needed anti-tetanus booster injections.

The Black Isle Show was lucky in hitting such a fine day and the crowd appeared to be a record one. On this, my first visit, I was greatly impressed with the slickness of the organisation of the day's events and congratulate all concerned. That show is particularly fortunate with their showyard and carparks being so free-draining. Less fortunate is the Haughs of Turriff, which as the very name indicates, is low-lying and liable to flood. Keith's soil is heavy clay and retains the water as the showgoers found to their cost this year.

Aren't we easily "hurtit" nowadays? A wee puckle mud on our shoes and we are moaning. Whereas those who can remember back to the Highland Show at Hazlehead, Aberdeen, before the show settled on a permanent site at Ingliston, will clearly remember what mud can be like. the glaur was so sticky that folk kept walking out of their wellingtons. Some of the cattle lines were complete quagmires and had to be abandoned.

At most of the shows, committees and exhibitors alike have been making an effort to increase the element of audience participation. the Highland and now the Black Isle had a highly successful food fair, where visitors could buy the produce of the area. Keith had an attractive children's farm where the bairns were encouraged to touch the calves and lambs. There were also piglets, hens, geese, ducks, rabbits and more.

But I particularly liked the Turriff Young Farmers' stand where the children had "hands on" participation. Boys were invited to bake scones and a simulated cow udder made from two calf feeders challenged the children to try their hand at milking. There was a time, a generation or so ago, when most folk had a granny or auntie who had a croft where they could work with the animals. Now their only opportunity to get close to farm animals occurs at agricultural shows and farm open days.

Although I haven't been getting on with the haymaking I haven't neglected the calving programme. August is the time of year when most of our heifers calve for the first time. In the space of one block of twenty-four hours we had seven calves. Some heifers take a short time from start to finish while others have a more protracted labour. Anyway, we give them constant attention and to date all goes well.

As it is still the school holidays the grandchildren are always ready to keep me company on my frequent walks through the cattle. We have a ford in the small burn that runs in the gulley between fields and often in summer it is little more than a trickle of water. This year, though, it is about twenty feet wide and maybe seven inches deep. There is a perfectly good footbridge as well but where is the fun in using a bridge when there is water to be plowtered in?

Grand-daughter number one is now eight and she waded through carefully with the water little more than halfway up her wellingtons. Grand-daughter number two is six and cautious by nature, so taking even greater care she got safely across, although the water came farther up her wellies.

Miss Bossy Boots, who is still waiting to be four, tries always to keep up with her sisters so nonchalently followed on in line. The water was crystal clear and she could see exactly where to put her feet. She made it fine to beyond half way but there the water was either too deep or her wellies were too short for they started to fill with very cold water.

The look of disbelief on her wee face was truly funny to see. Momentarily she thought of panicking but that would have meant losing face in front of her sisters. Instead she waded bravely on out of the burn and with a broad smile she proudly announced that her feet were very wet. It is a good job that Geraldine, their mother, keeps a "calm sough" and a good washing machine. Anyway, neither Miss BB nor I got a row. But there will be no more gallivanting or showgoing for the next sixteen days as Andy, our dairyman, is on holiday.

Here's hoping he gets at least some dry days. Maybe he is wise – or just fly – to choose the weeks when the breaking-in of the new heifers is at its height. It's a good job I like cows.

Groundwork pays dividends

I love this land!

It was while I was checking some heifers in calf in the worst field on the farm that I suddenly got a funny feeling. In the twelve years we have owned this farm the field in question has come on by leaps and bounds.

Before we bought it the entire farm had been growing only barley for eight years in succession. In that time all the straw had been baled and sold away. The fertility of the place was on a downward spiral and the yields of grain were getting less and less each year.

The sudden arrival of three hundred cattle of all ages must have been a big shock to the land, as well as to the worm and insect population on it. Throughout the winter period, when the cows are housed in cubicles and in straw-bedded courts, we estimate that the dung produced each day amounts to nine tons or thereby.

And for the past twelve years that quantity has been spread thickly on the stubble fields and ploughed in. In summertime, the grass fields which have been cut for hay or silage get a further light dressing to encourage regrowth. In a wet summer, such as we have just experienced, the strong smell of the fermented farmyard manure doesn't last long as the nutrients quickly get washed in by the rain.

As well as utilising all the grass and straw that the farm produces we also need to buy in about 1,000 big round bales to ensure that all the animals are comfortably bedded throughout the long winter period. This lasts about two hundred and twenty days in the case of the milking cows and maybe forty days less for the young stock.

We have deliberately avoided the use of slatted courts because of the problems of handling and spreading slurry. To counteract the acidifying effect of all the dung, we apply ground lime to the land to preserve the balance of ph as it is known. Barley, which is our main cereal crop, uses more lime than other cereals such as oats.

The agricultural colleges provide an excellent service, taking samples of soil from each field and analysing them for lime, potash and phosphate. Based on their results we apply fertilisers and trace elements to the crops.

For the first nine years, the soil seemed to absorb all the muck we could throw at it and hungered for more. After we had cut a grass crop for hay or silage, the fields looked parched and brown, and the aftermath, or second growth, was slow to get started. But three years ago, we began to see a difference. Where previously there had been a lot of bare ground when the grass was cut, now everything looked greener as the ground-hugging grasses thrive on the richness in the soil.

Now, this summer, even the poorest field, the one I was walking in, is showing considerable signs of improvement. I admit to feeling pleased with myself, seeing that our hard work has achieved results by bringing the farm up to its present state of fertility. On our farm, as on many other farms, the poorest fields are those farthest from the farm steading. In the days of horses and carts they didn't get their fair share of the muck midden.

On some of our better fields, though, the extra fertility is becoming an embarrassment. One field of barley in particular, has been over enriched.

This year the straw has grown soft and the crop is badly laid. Thank heavens for combine harvesters, which can pick up and thresh a badly-twisted crop. Back in the days of bindering, the lying holes had to be scythed out manually. Then the bouts of scythed barley had to be gathered into sheaves and bound by a cleverly made straw band. The art of making bands was one of the first skills that a harvest hand had to master, and women were regarded as the best bandsters.

I have always regretted that it was never my good fortune to share the pleasures of the harvest field with a bonny lassie.

When a field of barley gets badly laid, the underlying grass quickly grows up through the flattened barley straws and can clog the lifters and blades of the combine. This prevents the machine from making as good a job as it does in a standing crop. I can well remember the fierce arguments which used to go on, between the advocates and the opponents of combines, when these were coming into general use in the 1950s. "It could never make as clean a job as the binder", some said.

But these doubting Thomases have been proved completely wrong, as the modern combine does a far better job. Virtually all the grain is saved, whereas with bindering, stooking and double forking much more of the grain was shed than is now the case.

From the field I was in I could see three good crops, two of barley, one of wheat, which all promise to yield well. Romping round me were thirty-four heifers and a Limousin bull. They were looking exceptionally well, sleek and healthy. All things considered, I had no cause for complaint and I found myself expressing aloud, something I had known for a long time: "I love this land".

There was no one around to hear. If there had been somebody, I would probably have complained about the problems of too much fertility. After all, we must keep up the image of the North-east farmer – "aye girnin".

In the days when farms had big squads of men to work them, the youngest person on the farm, "the orra loon", was the butt for everybody's girnin.

One day, after a long spell of drought, the orra loon came out of the chaumer door to find the rain was pouring down. The first person he met was the farmer, whom he could never please, no matter how hard he tried.

"Aye aye, fermer. That's a fine shoor of rain. It will dae the neeps a lot o' guid", the lad said. "Ye muckle gype! The rain wid dae mair guid gin you would stan in at the stable door and let the watter fa' tae the grun, far it's meant tae gang", was the gruff reply.

Right now, thanks be, I am feeling fine, and have every intention of living a long time yet. But, as I was daundering through that park, enjoying my work, I thought perhaps this spot would be as good a place as any to have my ashes scattered, when my time finally comes.

I have only one other request to make. When the "boxie" comes back from the crematorium with the ashes, just scatter them!

Dinna send them to the college for analysis first!

Not just for Christmas

I am an avid reader of adverts. Especially the ones for livestock in the columns of *Farm Journal*.

But one I will not be responding to, is an advert for five-week-old turkey chicks – off heat. The way in which turkey farmers have managed to carve themselves a niche in today's meat market fills me with admiration. The blocks of turkey breast which are to be found in the cold-meat counters of our butchers shops and supermarkets are beautifully presented.

Turkey is no longer a meat eaten only at Christmas, although the five-week-old poults will have grown to handy weights by December and are obviously aimed at the festive dinner table.

It used to be the practice in our house to have hot roast turkey on Christmas Day and cold turkey for lunch next day. Then finally my sisters, brothers and I would have a session picking the carcase. We used to love that, delving our fingers into parts of the bone structure that knives couldn't reach.

The big chunks of meat were heaped on an ashet for converting into curried turkey, turkey fricassee or my special favourite, turkey vol-au-vents. The smaller bits went straight into our mouths. I guarantee there were no edible parts left on that frame after we vultures were through with it. But there was still goodness to be boiled out of the bones and the remains were consigned to the stock-pot.

Four days was about the maximum that turkey would be eaten in the space of a year. Then gradually, with the advent of deep-freezers, hotels began to offer it on the menu at weddings and such-like functions. Now turkey is no longer a luxury food and is available every day of the year in the form of cold cuts, steaks or drumsticks.

To have year-round availability you need to be hatching chicks all the time and not just in the spring and summer as in the past. The turkey hens must be persuaded to lay out of their natural season by artifically increasing the intensity of light.

I take my hat off to the specialists who work hard to ensure this all-year-round supply. Like so many other facets of agriculture, turkey-rearing has become a specialised job in the hands of a few experts.

Not all turkey meat has come from the "bootiful" man in Norfolk. Here in Grampian the long-established firm of Sorrie Brothers at Inverurie is currently in an expansionist phase. I wish Rosemary Sorrie every success with the turkey processing and packaging venture at Macduff. She certainly brings in the right kind of expertise to the business with her veterinary degree.

With today's high standards of hygiene at all stages of the growth of the birds, the need for using drugs has diminished. Turkey meat can claim to be as environmentally friendly as any other. It has the added advantage of being low in fat and high in protein.

I must be the world's worst turkey rearer. When I tried to raise them in the 1960s I thought I was doing the right thing by rearing them on fresh clean grass. I shifted the coop and wire run every second day. But still the creatures started to die on me. They just stood with their heads back and their mouths wide open.

I lost quite a few before I called in the expert, only to be told that they had been infected with gapes, a disease carried by the gape worm which is found in the soil. By providing what I considered a natural, fresh environment for my flock I had, in fact, hastened their demise.

I had bought the healthy fluffy little chicks as day-olds and put the fifty under five big broody hens in separate runs. By the time I changed the habitat, on the advice of the expert, and house them in a big shed, twenty or so had turned up their toes.

How turkeys ever survived as a species, even in the wild, quite escapes me. When it rained the daft things would start to queak loudly and kick up quite a din. They didn't have the wit to move ten inches to the pop-hole door of the hen house to get out of the wet. So a few more died of pneumonia.

Then their bonny red heads began to turn black and they went off their food. The dreaded scourge of turkeys, blackhead, was diagnosed, the only known cure at that time being small doses of arsenic in the drinking water. Chemists have a habit of looking askance at you when you go seeking arsenic or strychnine (for moles). By the time that outbreak halted and reversed there were less than twenty survivors – and the chemist was getting gey suspicious!

By Christmas we were left with the grand total of nine turkeys and I had taken orders for four times that so I had to buy in the market. I remember we ate a duck that year.

Having, as we thought, learned by our mistakes of the previous year we resolved to try again with five-week-olds the following year. 1964, I think it was, the wettest year ever. When the turkeys were half grown, we felt sorry for them being confined to the shed and started letting them outside during the day. The stronger birds took to roosting in trees and wouldn't be coaxed down, even on the wettest nights. The smaller ones had to be herded back to their shed before dark each night or they would huddle together for warmth and risk getting smothered.

Pneumonia struck again and we finished up with twenty. Half of these grew too big for the average household, which prefers a bird between eight and twelve pound, to fit the average kitchen oven. The bigger birds are favoured by hotels but command a smaller price.

Maybe I am too touchy about turkeys. Years later I was one of the eleven SNP Members of Parliament on the back benches, the night of the vote of no confidence in Jim Callaghan's government.

He was an ineffectual Prime Minister and had badly mishandled the "winter of discontent" but I had no wish to see his opponent, Mrs Thatcher, catapulted into office. I had some very bitter arguments with my colleagues about how we should vote.

In his winding-up speech, Jim Callaghan referred to the SNP members being "turkeys voting for Christmas". We were bringing on our own destruction, or words to that effect. It was true and I knew it. The subsequent election proved him to be absolutely right and the fact that we gave the country Thatcherism six months earlier than was necessary rankles with me even now.

So please! Don't ever "talk turkey" to me. I'm sensitive!

Claiking at Coliseum!

The wall I was leaning on was 2,000 years old, aye, and maybe more.

While my eyes were marvelling at the scene in front of me, my ears were listening intently to the words of the local Italian guide, who had enthralled us for two days with the fascinating history of her beloved Rome.

Then a voice that owed more to Turriff than to Tuscany broke through my revery with: "Aye aye, Hamish, fit are ye deeing here?" Then a few seconds later another Doric voice, this time from Elgin, chipped in: "I have often met you leaning over a ring, Hamish, but I didn't expect to see you at this one".

There we all were, marvelling at the enduring permanence of the Coliseum in Rome, when the two travel groups converged. For a few moments, we three North-easters exchanged greetings in the high-noon heat of the September day.

Each of us were thoroughly enjoying our late summer holiday, and were surprised to find Rome still so full of tourists. By that time of year, the Germans and French have all gone home, but the crowds of Brits and Japanese prefer to get around in the cooler weather of September and October.

This was now my third visit to Rome but that ancient city still gives me pleasure. Somehow, this time I was more bothered by the "piazza sairfeetie", than on previous occasions. I have heard it said, that the concrete, used by the Romans, sets harder with each passing year, and maybe that was the reason for my aching feet this time.

Three days is nowhere nearly long enough to see the marvels of the Eternal City and the tour operators set a very tight schedule. There is no time allowed for

lingering, or for "claiking" with lads from Turriff or Elgin, so we bid our hasty goodbyes and hurried after our respective groups.

The Thainstone mart complex at Inverurie, with its four acres of roof, looks big and busy on a Friday, with 2,500 cattle passing through and similarly on a Saturday with 15,000 sheep. But it pales into insignificance when you realise that 2,000 years ago the Coliseum needed 5,000 wild animals each feast day to keep the Roman crowds amused.

A long day's drive took us from Rome to the Bay of Naples, through a truly spectacular countryside. There seemed to be even more roadworks going on in Southern Italy than there had been in the North.

The new roads under construction will, undoubtedly, speed up communications. I doubt, however, if belting down a straight motorway will hold the same fascination as driving round hairpin bends, crossing deep gorges and disappearing into unexpected tunnels. I only know I wouldn't have wished to miss one mile of that intensely interesting journey.

When you see all the thousands of tiny vineyards clinging to the sides of impossibly steep hillsides, it becomes clear how the EC has such a huge wine lake. And yet, no bureaucrat should seek to deny anyone the right to drink the wine of their own locality. I am becoming firmly convinced that the Common Market will survive only if each member nation is held responsible for its own food surpluses, and wine and tobacco should be excluded from subsidy payments.

The dairy expansion which I mentioned last week is very evident from the road, with the newly-built cattle barns conspicuous on the "the breist o' the brae". The long low sheds are situated near the ridge of a slope where they can catch every breeze that blows, to keep the cows cool in summer. I noted too, that they have adopted the Israeli practice of planting small clumps of trees at either end of the buildings to stimulate air currents.

Here and there small herds of beef cattle could be seen grazing on exceptionally steep pastures. And just occasionally, a herd of black water buffaloes, whose milk makes the best mozzarella cheese, were feeding on land near rivers.

These animals are heavier than the average cow, with strong bones and a thick hide. I would have loved to stop and inquire about their husbandry, as I understand the buffalo need to wallow in water at least once a day. Perhaps a modern sprinkler system has the same effect, but as I was the only farmer in the entire coach party and our driver was a "townie", I had no way in finding out.

Mozzarella is sold in all food shops and, for all the earth, it reminds me of badly shaped tennis balls. When fresh, the texture is rubbery, but when it has dried out after a few weeks, the cheese balls become really hard. They are then grated finely and the powdered cheese is sprinkled on pasta to give it some taste.

When in Rome do as the Romans' is a well-kent saying, so I faithfully ate pasta once, on each of the fourteen days. They can call it what they like, spaghetti, macaroni, ravioli, gnocchi, or anything else, it is still pasta and completely tasteless.

Each dish depends on the filling and the grated cheese to give them flavour. I, personally, would rather have porridge or brose or skirlie or even mealie jimmies, for these get at least some flavour from the oatmeal.

Now that I have sampled the Italian efforts, I will better appreciate my own making of macaroni and cheese, with bacon, mushrooms and tomatoes for a filling. But, as my mother was fond of saying: "Kale at hame is nae kitchie". Roughly translated, that means "Food at home is not appreciated". Well, it is now!

Several of my fellow trippers succumbed to tummy upsets and I took great pleasure in introducing them to the sure Scots cure. Five spoonfuls of sugar round the rim of a small plate. Pour on enough good whisky to moisten the sugar thoroughly. Warm the mixture under a grill until hot. Then strike two matches to set the whisky alight.

Let it burn like a Christmas pudding until it goes out, allow to cool slightly, then sup the mixture with a spoon. Never mind the shudders, keep supping, the taste will grow on you. Go promptly to bed. You will be asleep within fifteen minutes and will wake up in the morning refreshed and completely cured.

I went on to explain that when I was a child, we ignited the mixture with a red hot poker heated in a peat fire, but the grill does the job just as well. I couldn't, unfortunately, tell them which whisky burns best.

A delightful couple from Wales collared me at breakfast one morning. "There is only one thing wrong with your cure, Hamish" complained the husband.

"And what is that?" I queried, quite indignant that my remedy should be called into question.

"Well, your medicine is so effective, that I have no excuse to try it again tonight".

Wee drams with Sir Harold . . .

I liked Harold Wilson. And what was more important – he liked me.

The determination of political journalists to find something sinister about Sir Harold has always puzzled me and I can certainly claim to have known him far better than either of the authors of two books reviewed by Bill Howatson in the *Press and Journal* last Saturday.

Friendship between a lowly back-bencher and a Prime Minister was perhaps unusual and I valued our times together more than any other experience in my five years as an MP. As I was neither a member of his own Labour Party, nor of his principal opposition, he felt he could relax in my company – and frequently did. I knew him both while he was in the driving seat for two years and also after he had resigned through chronic ill-health and gone to the back benches.

Our friendship started during the short Parliament which lasted from February to October, 1974. As the only businessman in our small group of seven SNP members, I was landed with the job of treasurer. We had no kitty from the party in Scotland and yet we desperately needed a paid office manager.

There was talk, just talk that the Government was contemplating giving money to Opposition parties in the House, so I sought audience with the top of the tree, the Prime Minister himself. My able colleague Douglas Henderson, the then member for East Aberdeenshire and I duly presented ourselves at the PM's office in the Commons one evening.

Mrs Marcia Williams, Mr Wilson's political secretary, offered us a whisky and proceeded to quiz us about the political situation in Scotland. We were both impressed by her detailed knowledge of virtually every seat and by the almost uncanny accuracy of her assessment of the course of future voting patterns. She also proved of immense help in pointing us in the right direction for office equipment. When Mr Wilson arrived some twenty minutes late, he was most affable, and completely devoid of arrogance. Our request for financial help was well documented and he quickly accepted the validity of our argument.

He promised to consult with the leader of the House, Mr Edward Short and arranged a subsequent meeting, again in his office. We enlisted the support of the Liberals, the Ulster Unionists and the Welsh Nationalists on a joint approach. Mr Short also agreed the good sense of our submission and today the money for opposition parties is known as "the Short Money".

Harold Wilson appreciated a dram of good malt whisky, although I would strongly refute the suggestion made by his detractors, that he was ever a heavy drinker. Subsequently, I would call at his office, sometimes summonsed from the Chamber by Mrs Williams, and we would spend the hour or so before the ten o'clock vote sipping our one glass of whisky.

There are around thirty distilleries in Banffshire, all making fine whiskies and I would hand in a bottle to the PM's office, knowing that I would be invited to taste it before long. I sometimes did the same with Fred Peart who was arguably the finest Minister of Agriculture Britain has ever had. I did not succeed in getting the lime subsidy restored, but it wasn't for the lack of trying.

Occasionally I would meet Harold in the evening after he had entertained trade unionists to midnight beer and sandwiches at No. 10. He would shake his head at the intransigence of the union leaders who thought their sole purpose in life was to win ever larger pay packets for their members, regardless of the profitability of their company.

As an economist himself, he worried about the competitiveness of British industry. He could see the threat from Japan and Korea to our shipbuilding industry. Harold Wilson never really recovered from the destruction of Barbara Castle's bill, "In Place of Strife", which had sought to curb the worst excesses of trade union power and to modernise industrial practices. Jim Callaghan had been anxious to curry favour with the unions and had failed to give the bill his backing.

Mr Wilson was a worrier and often didn't sleep well. There were times when he was too exhausted to speak but I could get him to relax by asking about his family in Western Australia, and he also liked to talk of his childhood. He was not good at delegating and was far too lenient with the union bosses who would bypass the appropriate minister and insist on going direct to No. 10. Neither was he a tough guy and he gave in to their demands far too often.

It was only after Mrs Thatcher became Leader of the Opposition that Mr Wilson's mental exhaustion became obvious. Where previously he had, with a scathing tongue, bested Edward Heath at Question Times, he couldn't do the same with Mrs Thatcher.

This used to puzzle me until one day in the chamber the answer came to me. Mr Wilson could not be nasty to a woman. Some of his own left wing women MPs, such as Judith Hart, Renee Short and Audrey Wise, were downright rude to him. Yet he would never retaliate and slap them down as he would his male colleagues.

Then, a few months later, he would occasionally lose the thread of his argument at the dispatch box and leave himself completely vulnerable. By this time, he had told me confidentially of his intention to retire in the near future. I urged him to get it over quickly as I hated seeing him being ill-used.

Although Mr Wilson was no farmer, he was amused at my analogy when I said: "If I had a sick stirk being bullied in the way you are, I would have removed it from the cattle court long before this". I was relieved to see him go, as he would certainly have collapsed if he had remained in office much longer.

Harold Wilson was, in my estimation, a fair man who had the stuffing knocked out of him by unfair politicians, unfair trade unionists and sleekit civil servants, who lacked vision and were fearful of change.

Young ones make mark

Miss Bossy Boots likes the school!

Now that she is four and a fully-enrolled pupil at the nursery school she has holidays, the same as her big sisters, and this is important.

Because the entire month of October has been so wet, I still haven't lifted my tatties, all four drills of them in the back garden. I had intended to enlist the help of the girls and so give them some understanding of the real meaning of the "tattie holidays".

Mind you, this traditional holiday is more often given the posh title of "mid-term break" nowadays, for such it has become, now that giant potato harvesters have replaced the squads of school children of yesteryear. Although there were no tatties to lift and rain was pelting down each day, Valerie turned out for her "work" clad in boiler suit and wellies, with that ready smile on her face.

When I was a wee loon, my mother used to tell me I had a tongue that could "clip cloots". Now I know of someone else who fits the same description. The lass never stops asking questions, and needs sensible answers, before moving on to the next subject. Sometimes we can see the wee soul thinking – and reasoning.

On one of the many wet days Michael and I had been de-horning calves and we had abandoned the holding crate in the passage between the pens. Coming and going, we had squeezed past the thing for several days, until Valerie could stand it no longer. "That crate shouldn't be there, Grandpa", she announced, "you should shift it to another shed, out of the way". And, of course, she was dead right, so we rather sheepishly obeyed orders and moved the obstacle.

Anouther day, Valerie was helping Andy, our dairyman, to shift a four-day-old Limousin from the calving box into a fresh calf pen. Lots of calves are lively at this stage, but we find that Limousin calves are just like deer – they will hardly stay in a pen, and can scramble over the high walls no bother.

When this particular calf had jumped loose for the third time Andy gave it a good swearing. Valerie, who had left the calf pen this time, heard Andy holding forth. She came back to the shed and said quietly, "Now Andy! That's enough! Daddy just puts that old door on to keep the calfie in". Her Daddy had, in fact, done it only once, but the significance had not been lost on the wee lass.

The cats which get milk twice daily in the calf shed are real farm cats. They are quiet enough to feed among our feet but are spitfires if we try to touch them. Usually quick to stick their claws in, they allow Miss BB to lift and cuddle them with impunity.

The children's special cat, Mandy, is about twelve years old, so far as we know. She came to the farm as a stray kitten shortly after we moved here. The old puss is now the grandmother and great-grandmother of this year's brood of kittens.

She even had three herself in May. Normally, Mandy rears her off-spring in the shed where the big bales of hay are stored. But for some reason she carried them to the door of the house this year, as if knowing the three little girls would take pity on them. She was right, of course. Mandy and her family had to have a comfortable box in the hallway, a warm blanket and tit-bits from the kitchen table.

Giant potato harvesters have replaced the squads of school children of yesteryear

From day one, these kittens have been cuddled and coo-ed over every time the girls go in or out of the house. Now the brutes are well-grown and have no fear of anyone. Unlike the farm cats they don't know when to keep out of the way, and are constantly among our feet.

The other day I was fixing a jack to change a punctured wheel on a bogey. One kitten just wouldn't stay away from my hands and when I finally gave it a good biff it jumped on my shoulder and dug ints claws into my neck.

Any day now an advert will appear in the local paper – "Free to good homes. Lovely house-trained kittens". Even Valerie agrees they have out-grown their box and out-stayed their welcome.

Everybody has heard of "wetting the baby's head" when there is a new arrival in a family. Well! Here on the farm we are wetting the calfie's head.

Many moons ago, maybe twenty-five years to be more precise, the Scottish and English milk marketing boards imported a young Candian Holstein bull called Linmac. It turned out a tremendous improver of the British Friesian breed and sired many thousands of excellent cows through the artificial insemination service. After the bull died the price of the few remaining straws of semen rocketed to more than £100 per straw.

My good friend and long-time rival, Tom Robertson of Piriesmill at Huntly, had still one straw left and I acquired it when he decided to give up dairying. Linmac was not a Holstein of the extreme type, unlike some of the greyhounds which have been imported since then, and it added size and stature to the breed.

For the last five years we have cherished this straw in our deep-freeze tank, waiting for the right cow to be the recipient. The bonny Dutch type Friesian which we chose had milked well in her first two lactations and she comes of a family of cows known for their longevity. By great good luck, the insemination, carried out by Michael proved successful and hurdle number one was over – the cow was in calf to her one and only service.

Six months later, the vet diagnosed her pregnancy and all was well. Between Andy, Michael and myself, we pay a lot of attention to our calving cattle and check them frequently. Andy was the first to spot that the cow had started calving. Closer inspection revealed that the one foot showing was a hind foot but he soon brought the other one forward.

Often a cow can make little progress with a breach birth so he fetched the calving machine and attached the ropes to the calf's ankles. All went well and Andy quickly had a living calf blinking its eyes amongst the straw.

By jabbing a straw up its nose Andy got the calf breathing and hurdle number two was past. Soon the strong bull calf had struggled to its feet and started to suckle its mother. And now, provided we can avoid pneumonia, and scour, and vitamin deficiencies, we should have a young stock bull ready to work some fifteen months from now.

Is it too much to hope that he will pass on to his progency, the fleshing quality of his mother and the heavy milking qualities and the extra size from his father's family? We will have to wait another five years to find out.

When there are young animals and young children around the farm each day is an adventure. Doubtless, in a few days, Miss Bossy Boots will be keeping us all right as we endeavour to rear young Linmac successfuly.

Cheers!

North call for winning event

I never need a second bidding to go to Caithness.

And when the Latheron Agricultural Society invited me to give the address at its annual dinner and presentation of trophies, I was delighted to oblige.

November the fifth was a lovely day all day, so I took the afternoon off work to travel north in daylight. After seeing the thousands of acres of straw still to be baled in Aberdeenshire the previous day, it was great to see that every farmer along the Moray firth, the Black Isle and Easter Ross had completed the harvest. Widely-scattered sheep were now gleaning the stubble fields.

The last of our own harvest had been combined the night before. The oats were just too flat for the combine to lift and most of it still remains on the ground. The big baler could not differentiate between the combined straw and the uncut stuff. It kept clogging, with inches of earth gathering on the rollers.

As the oat field is definitely the last one to bale for this year, the task of cleaning the machine prior to laying up for the winter needs to be done quickly before the mud dries – but not by me this time. The task of gleaning the long oat straw will be given to some strong in-calf heifers.

As I took the road, the bright sunny day put a glow on the countryside – this is the time of year when the larch trees come into their own with their many shades of gold. When I reach Evanton nowadays I am faced with the dilemma of which route to take. The new crossings of the Dornoch Firth, beyond Tain, cuts more than twenty miles off the journey. But, for scenery, these twenty miles over the Struie hill take a bit of beating.

Where thirty years ago there were only barren moors, now thousands of acres of thriving woodlands give promise of jobs to come. The trees are at varying stages of growth and have a good mix of species, providing food and shelter for a variety of birdlife. The view from the top of Struie looking west to the Kyles of Sutherland and Bonar Bridge never ceases to delight me.

I first got to know Sutherland and Caithness when I was cutting my political teeth as a Tory candidate way back in the 60s. I didn't come across many Tories but I met a lot of the fine folk of all political persuasions. In the by-going, I became familiar with most of the hirsels of North Country Cheviot sheep in those two vast counties, and the knowledge has stood me in good stead at sheep sales down the years.

It is a pity that sheep don't have votes. These had to be gleaned from the towns and villages, and there is hardly a street in Caithness where I haven't knocked on some doors or a village hall where I haven't addressed a meeting. Speakers are rarely aware of their mannerisms and I was blissfully ignorant of mine until the day my daughters accompanied me to three meetings in the Lybster district.

At the second meeting I could see Lorna, the younger of the two, smiling and at the third meeting she and her sister, Maureen, could hardly keep from laughing. "What did you find so amusing?" I asked in the car afterwards.

"Oh! Daddy!" giggled Lorna, "You have no idea how many scones you baked at that last meeting!" If I still have mannerisms, at least the good folk of Latheron didn't laugh at them last week but rather they laughed with me.

However, my use of a good Scots word didn't amuse show secretary Mrs Patricia Heggs! When I phoned her prior to the dinner she mentioned that she was from south of the border and her accent was somewhat different from the other show committee members. I jokingly remarked "You will be something of a kenspeckle figure then". It was meant as a compliment, but as she couldn't find the word in the dictionary she had her doubts! I assured her later, the word "kenspeckle" means "easily recogniseable".

The Latheron Agricultural Society has a tremendous array of trophies and many of the winners were at the dinner to receive them personally. Others could not be there for varying reasons and many will receive their awards by the hand of a truly kenspeckle and popular character, "A. I." Willie.

Because his job of artificial inseminator takes him all over both counties, Willie MacKay seems to have become somthing of a general factotum. He is just the kind of obliging person a widely-scattered community comes to rely on, and he is obviously held in very high regard. In my address, I praised the way in which local agricultural shows have helped to foster quality in the cattle and sheep stocks of the area. I asked the Caithness audience to put greater faith in quality stock than in the promise of politicians.

Within three years the Common Agricultural Policy will, I believe, be in crisis and may well be abandoned. Regardless of the individual quota allocated, it is important that each producer keeps his stock numbers up. Quality cattle and sheep will always be in strong demand even though they are over and above the number eligible for subsidy. Our abattoirs need the throughput and Europe is fast learning to appreciate the taste of Scots quality meat.

At the dinner, I enjoyed what was perhaps the most succulent piece of roast beef I have ever tasted. That dish and the friendliness of my Caithness hosts alone made the long journey north worthwhile. I had intended spending the weekend exploring the many small harbours down the rocky East Coast, but sadly with mist and rain closing in next morning I reluctantly curtailed my visit.

Just as in Burghead or Portsoy or Banff the big old warehouses at the harbours tell of a thriving past, before the advent of road and rail transport. It would be fascinating to lay hands on a manifest of a boat calling at these small ports two centuries ago. In Norse times Caithness was known as the granary of the North Atlantic. Grain from there was shipped to Norway, Faroe and Iceland as well as to nearby Shetland and the Western Isles.

The amount of grain grown in Caithness nowadays would not fill many boats. On the other hand, the quality and quantity of today's beef and lamb is undoubtedly the highest ever. The one thing Caithness does not need is conservationists. Much of the bare moorland would certainly benefit from a generous planting of mixed conifers to act as a wind-break and provide shelter for both man and beast.

Equally, another thing that Caithness does not require is somebody from south of the Ord telling them what to do!

Washing out blues

The unmistakable smell of a burned-out electric motor greeted me as I walked into the kitchen the other day.

With ten years constant use and only one repair, the old washing machine had given good service and I had no cause for complaint. There was nothing for it but to let the moths fly from my wallet and fork out for a new one. Seeing all the sophisticated electronic models in the showroom set me thinking of the washing days of my youth.

As in most hoseholds, Monday was set aside for the heaviest work of the week and cooking had to take second place. Milk and rice soup was never my favourite dish but I knew better than complain. The first washing machine I remember was a clumsy wooden affair that occupied a whole corner of our large kitchen. Although it was only a slightly mechanised wash-tub, it was nevertheless an advance on the old plumper with the three-legged dolly which stirred the clothes.

Many examples of the plumper barrel can still be found in farm and cottage museums, in fact I saw one at the Laidhay Croft Museum in Caithness recently, but I have never come across another similar to the one my mother used. The ungainly wooden contraption, which stood on four legs, had to be filled and emptied by means of large ladles. Heavy black pots, which hung on the sway over the peat fire, provided a seemingly endless supply of boiling water to fill the cavernous belly of the machine.

Then, half a bar of yellow paraffin soap was flaked into the tub and the lid fastened securely. The heavy wooden handle with arms at both ends was pushed and pulled alternately. The movement turned two paddles which tumbed the clothes round and round. With small items it was hard work but with heavy items like blankets and dairy overalls it needed the strength of Hercules. I always thought that on washdays the womenfolk worked harder than the men outside in the fields and they certainly worked longer hours.

Each fill of water was used twice before emptying – first the dirty clothes and then the very dirty clothes. The tub had no tap or hose and the soapy water was laboriously ladled into pails and carried outside to the nearest ditch for disposal. In the spring and summer it was carried to the garden to check the carrot fly or the caterpillars. Close by the kitchen door grew the healthiest bush of flowering currant I have ever seen.

No fly or aphid could survive the constant washday drenching. We bairns did our best to keep out of the kitchen for the womenfolk were apt to be short of temper and a cheeky little loon just invited a wet cloth round his bare legs. No cowboy with a lasso was ever as accurate as my mother. She could hit the backs of knees with unerring aim every time I came within range and it sure was nippy.

The drudgery was made only slightly less with the arrival a few years later, of the latest wonder – a Jiffy washing machine. We required the biggest size and if I stood on a stool I could just swing the handle on its wide 180 degrees arc. Although it still needed to be filled from the big pots, it had a tap and a hose which carried the waste water to the nearest drain.

At first the Jiffy had a hand-wringer which used to break shirt and blouse buttons, but soon it was replaced by an Acme electric one, which did less damage and was the first real labour-saving device in our kitchen. Of course, very heavy articles still had to go through the big wooden rollered mangle, and that required a lot of effort.

Just prior to the outbreak of World War II, farmers began to get better prices for their produce. We could now afford a shining new Aga cooker with its inbuilt hot water system so now both intake and outlet to the washing machine was by hose. Only the carrying of the clothes baskets to the drying green remained heavy work and the bairns were invited to take an end.

The clothes ropes were parallel to the farm road and the drystane dyke between the two was a mass of marigolds and "snow in summer". The flowers attracted hundreds of bees from the hives nearby so it wasn't a place to linger long.

But I really got "the washday blues" one Monday when I was about nine. I was getting too big for blouses and jerseys and had set my heart on acquiring a jacket. When an aunt gave me a birthday present of a brown corduroy jerkin with a zip front I thought "I was Erchie".

In the mid 30s, zips were still very new and something of a rarity. None of my sisters had clothes with a zip so I was really proud of my new possession. Although I kept it for best, the jerkin soon got dirty and had to be washed – and that was its downfall.

Today we have cows and especially calves, which develop a craving for chewing plastic baler twine, and we try to remove it from their mouths whenever possible. But back then, the craving was for coir yarn, binder twine or hessian sacks. One good brown cow was notorious for chewing cloth of any kind and occasionally a dish towel would be missed from the washline.

If the bees hadn't been there we children would have been more ready to chase the cow away from the washing green as she passed on her way to the byre. On the day in question, the bold lady took a fancy to my jerkin and no one saw her pull it from the line. We hunted high and low for the garment and that night I went to bed "gey doon in the moo". Next morning, there in the manger in front of the cow, was the clear evidence – a neatly regurgitated zip with just a few strands of corduroy to prove its origin.

My aunt was never told of the ignominious end of her present and I never had another jerkin. The cow lived and produced well for many years but she fortunately confined her cravings to sacking after that. Needless to say she acquired the title of "chaw cloots" and equally needless to say, I never forgave her.

With the advent of mechanisation on the farm, fewer and fewer staff were needed, and besides, the family grew up and went away as families always do. As a consequence, the size of the weekly wash diminished and was mechanised too with the advent of the electric washing machine. The worst of the hard work had gone from washing day.

Although in her later years my mother appreciated the latest labour-saving models, she was horrified at the amount of water used by the fully-plumbed-in machines. My new acquisition is, however, more ecologically friendly and hopefully will reduce my water meter charges too.

By the way, did I ever tell you about the time I boiled my Air Force issue woollen socks – and ended up on a charge?

It's mud, mud, glaur-iest mud!

Plowter, plowter, plowter. If it doesn't rain during the day it rains all night. And nothing gets a chance to dry. This has without doubt been the wettest autumn and early winter in the last twelve years.

To get away from dubs, we moved from a heavy-land farm to a lighter, drier soil near the coast. Until now, we have appreciated the improvement – but the past fourteen weeks have been both a nightmare and a quagmire. Like most other North-east farmers we have had a tyuave getting the harvest finished. Much of our grain is of inferior quality and will prove difficult to sell.

Fortunately, with our heavy stockings of cattle and sheep, we consume most of our grain at home. Usually we have our wheat sold by this time, but here we are still struggling to get the moisture content down. There just hasn't been a long enough spell of dry weather to blast dry air through the bins and harden up the grain.

Where is the point in using the heaters if all we do is blow warm air of high humidity? With constant turning we can keep it cool but, to date, the final few degrees of drying evades us. Any day now the bill for electricity will come through the letter box with a heavy thump. I envy anyone who bought Hydro-Electric shares – I will be paying their dividend this quarter.

We grew a great crop of kale for the dairy cows this year. The wet summer suited the crop and, with the field being close to the steading, we looked forward to an easy time. Letting the cows graze a strip of kale for a couple of hours per day helps to keep down feeding costs. That is the theory but this year the practice has been very different.

Trying to choose two dry hours during daylight is a lottery. Cows do not like driving rain and they will stand in a corner with their backs to the storm rather than go grazing. As a result the kale is lasting far longer than usual. Even when it does stop pouring, the cows have to plunge through the muddy ground to get to the fresh break of kale beneath the electric fence. What is usually a dry, free-draining field has deteriorated into a sea of gutters.

Although I am not normally someone who wishes my life away, I would be very happy to see that crop finished and have the cows housed up for the rest of the winter. The present situation reminds me of my late colleague, Donald Stewart, MP for the Western Isles. Donald was a great wit and occasionally he would be sipping a pint of beer and making a face. "This is terrible beer" he would say, "I'll be right glad when it is finished". Well, I am getting to that stage with the kale.

If only the mud would stay in the field it might not be so bad, but even the concrete roads round the steading get clarted practically every day. Thank goodness for the tractor-mounted squeegee which scrapes the surfaces, for I had my share of "swiping dubs" with besoms when I was a youth. My father had a fetish for it. But we still have the task of loading the liquid mud and spreading it back on a drier grass field wherever a tractor and spreader can get footing.

Working hard and getting nowhere is a phenomenon that happens to everyone once in a while. That is the treadmill we are on right now. Andy, the dairyman, has not a lot to smile about at the moment as he has to double wash, and wipe every

teat to get it mud-free before he puts the clusters on the cows. No matter how busy, he still has a laugh a d a cheery banter with Miss Bossy Boots as she sets off each afternoon with her dad to shift the electric fence. If the wee lass can keep in the dry ground among the fresh kale stalks, she manages. But when she gets stuck fast in soft stuff, she just stands there and shouts for help.

Only when Valerie walks out of a wellie and her stockinged foot squelches in the glaur do the tears appear. Once she reaches the hard road, she makes a beeline to splash in the deep puddles, soaking herself even more, and says with a smile "I'm just cleaning my wellies".

Have you ever noticed that dubs have a funny way of working up the inside of each wellie leg as one leg passes the other? Maybe that explains why farmers walk the way they do! But I'm truly grateful that I don't have a one hundred strong herd of sows running out of doors on the kennel system. Those farmers must be facing appalling difficulties getting their sows fed and watered. Often the tractors get bogged down just trying to reach the feed troughs. The pigs have so churned up the surface with their snouts in their search for roots among the divots, that there is no hard surface left for the wheels to get a grip.

The people who shout loudest for keeping sows outdoors should get the jobs of carrying pails of food to the pig arks for just one day. Then they would be the first to shout "Get these poor wretched animals inside!" And I am doubly glad that I no longer keep hens on free range. Even the finest strain of pullets would be off the lay after twelve weeks of being buffeted by wind and drenched by rain. And pity too, the poor henwife who has to struggle against the gale twice each day with food for the miserable birds, plowtering through the gutters as she does so.

The much loved North-east poet J. C. Milne summed the whole situation up beautifully:

Och aye, Jean hersel'. Awa oot bye, wi the orra pail.
Danced at Kings. Took a good degree.
Kent maist things, but what she'd be.
She's mistress noo at Futretsprot.
A fermtoun life – the scunner o't.

Scunner or no, we'll jist hae tae plowter on. At least the Gatt negotiations haven't got bogged down and so a fierce trade war with the US has been averted. So, thankfully, we have one bright note to end an otherwise dreich year. My dreams for a white Christmas have come true. It's cleaner!